Then He Stepped In

by

Diane Dybus

RoseDog✿Books

PITTSBURGH, PENNSYLVANIA 15222

The contents of this work including, but not limited to, the accuracy of events, people, and places depicted; opinions expressed; permission to use previously published materials included; and any advice given or actions advocated are solely the responsibility of the author, who assumes all liability for said work and indemnifies the publisher against any claims stemming from publication of the work.

RoseDog Books
701 Smithfield Street
Pittsburgh, PA 15222
Visit our website at *www.rosedogbookstore.com*

ISBN: 978-1-4349-7323-8
eISBN: 978-1-4349-2034-8

PREFACE

This book was written to give glory and thanksgiving to God. I have witnessed everything personally and my hope is that it will encourage you that our needs will be fulfilled through faith in Jesus Christ.

I have dedicated this book to my granddaughter, Lauryn, who never ceases to ask me to tell her one more story, whether it be morning, noon, or night. I want her and my other grandchildren to understand throughout their lives that nothing is impossible with the Lord- absolutely nothing!

Diane Dybus

God has given Diane a mighty ministry of love and compassion. For several years Diane was our music director at the Bethpage Assembly of God Church. Each time she led our congregation in worship, the presence of God in the person of the Holy Spirit was so magnificent and powerful

In every service, hundreds of people were blessed, lifted and moved as she lovingly and courageously encouraged the people to believe for miracles. Many have testified of healing and deliverance as a result of her anointed ministry. Since Diane came to know Christ nearly 50 years ago she has passionately impacted our world with the touch of God.

-Rev. Sal Bennardo
Senior Pastor- Bethpage Assembly of God Church.

Diane Dybus is the premier classical music piano teacher on Long Island having a career spanning nearly 50 years. Trained at the Manhattan School of Music and playing piano at Carnegie Hall and on radio since she was a young girl, she is a tour de force of personality and charm. Diane is also a highly regarded NYSSMA judge and many of her own students go on to win high awards for their performances and musical accomplishments. She is much more than an academic, however. As a teacher and involved mentor, Diane has intimately impacted the lives of literally thousands of students and their families though her personal testimonies of extraordinary miracles she has experienced in her life through her unshakable faith in God. As a woman of deep Christian faith, Diane believes that no problem is too large or too small for God to intervene if you would just invite him to bring meaning, healing and restoration to the situation. She is always ready to pray with and pray for those with whom she comes into daily contact. The results speak for themselves...LIFE CHANGING MIRACLES!

Diane is not without having experienced her own personal tragedies, however. Her only son, Ricky, died unexpectedly in his sleep at the young age of 21 years in 1988. Undeterred in her faith in God, Diane has brought hope, encouragement and healing to others in similar situations. She is an indefatigable and compassionate warrior for suffering people wherever she goes including her many students and even people with whom she comes into only casual contact, offering a surprising word of hope or encouragement wherever she goes.

Many of the factual stories you will read about in this book will seem to be too far fetched to be believable. That is what makes Diane's life and her testimonies so compelling. With strong faith in the God who has all power over his creation, Diane believes (and is eager to share this with others) that God is on your side and that "prayer changes things" if you would just be so bold as to ask, in faith, believing, as the Bible says. "Nothing is impossible to those who believe," is certainly her life's motto.

When Diane is not teaching piano and encouraging and praying for others she can usually be found tending her gigantic collection of plants or reading her Bible with her husband and soul mate of over 50 years, Tony.

Read this book and be encouraged to trust God for the seemingly impossible!

-Daniel Buttafuoco

I began writing this book many years ago, but I put down the pen when my twenty-one year old son unexpectedly, in his sleep, went home to be with the lord. His healing at birth changed my life forever and the lives of my family. The pain of his death is really not describable. The Lord taught me, the only way to get through such grief is to take your mind off yourself and encourage other people that they can make it through any adversity with Gods help. Thus the reason for this book.

Looking Back

Although I was raised a Catholic, educated in grammar and high school at a Catholic institution, God was really not part of my life. I can't ever remember speaking about Jesus in our house. I can't recall ever praying over our food or acknowledging God was in our lives. Going to church was a habit. If you didn't go it was a Mortal sin and no one wanted that on our soul.

The Beginning of Gods Intervention

My Mom suffered from ringing in her ears for years and years. She was constantly complaining about it. Then one day upon leaving church she said to me as she was coming down the steps, "Jesus just healed my ears." As simple as that! No fanfare, no excitement. It certainly startled me! Wonderful! God can heal today? How awesome is that, I thought.

A Dream From Above

One day when I was about twelve years old, my mom told me about a dream she had the night before. She dreamt she died and she sat on her coffin looking at the people at her funeral. Then she said she found herself in a long line. She came up to a tall man with long golden hair and a golden colored robe. He said, "I'll take you" and put his hand on her upper chest area. She showed me where he touched her and found the fingerprints were totally visible on her skin. We thought by the end of the day they would have disappeared, but they remained there for weeks. My brother began telling neighbors and people would come to our house to hear the story and see the fingerprints. I began to think that maybe God was real! I began a prayer life, which I never had before saying many Our Fathers, Hail Marys and Acts of Contrition, any prayer that I could find; I became interested in God and wanted to know Him.

The Beginning of my Career

I began taking piano lessons at the age of five. My father's sister was a pianist who played background music for the old silent movies. My dad played the Violin. My parents decided I would be a musician.

I started competing and performing at an early age. I entered a Lions Club competition; The first prize was money and a chance to play solo on W.K.B.S. radio, Oyster Bay. In those days that was a tremendous honor. I prayed to win and God answered. I was asked to continue to play, which I did, every Saturday morning for many months. My husband was forced to listen to me play one Saturday by his mother when I was 10 years old. Little did he know that someday I would be his wife. It's all in God's plan.

Competitions

I was entered in a contest in a movie theatre in Connecticut where our relatives lived. My uncle was always very proud of me. I wanted to win for him because he cared so much about my talent. After I played Malaguena, I went out on the fire escape and prayed to win. I thought it was impossible as others were much more impressive than I was. I did win. I was very excited and I started to build a faith in God that grew to this day. I continued to compete in many competitions. I played solo and also played with another very talented girl, on two pianos. We competed in an organization called the Music Education League. It encouraged young people to compete for gold medals and for the winners to perform at various recital halls in the city. As a duo we won many times, and I won also as a soloist. I brought home many gold medals. Looking back, I realize that my talent had also come from the Lord above. I just didn't realize it then. He gave me a gift.

The First New York Meeting

When I was fifteen my parents took me to a New Years dance. There I met the man I would marry. He was in the service at that time. Our families knew each other. He came back after the dance to our house. I told my mom he would be the man I would marry. I loved him the first time I saw his face. We corresponded while he was in Europe. When he returned we were in his sister's wedding party together. It was the start of what would be a long long relationship. We are now approaching our 51st wedding anniversary.

We were married when I just turned nineteen, and I was still pursuing my musical career at the Manhattan School of Music in New York City. It was difficult traveling in and out of the city each day on subways and trains because I became pregnant with our first daughter immediately after our wedding.

The First Child

Nine months and two days after our marriage I gave birth. It was a very difficult delivery, and I was in labor two full days. When the doctor finally induced the baby she split my cervix open. From so much pressure on her head, the doctors were worried about brain damage. Again the Lord watched over us. She came home from the hospital healthy and strong, and now has three beautiful daughters of her own.

Our Second Child

Three years later, I gave birth to another daughter, Laurie, and I had begun a wonderful teaching career with a small studio in my house in Levittown. It certainly helped with paying our bills. We weren't rich, that was for sure. We owed thousands of dollars to the college, but God provided and we were content and happy. I was ecstatic that we owned our own home as humble as it was.

God was always there but sort of in the background of our lives. We went to church, we believed, but there was really no true relationship with the creator. It was just what we were supposed to do-a habit.

The Bible

Then one day something happened that changed my life. I came home from shopping and my husband said, " I bought you something." I was very excited only to learn that he bought a bible from a vendor going door to door, I was angry because money was scarce. He gave a down payment of five dollars and I had to pay the rest. I thought to myself " Why would we ever read a bible?" It was never opened, it laid there on the table for months.

A Miscarriage

I became pregnant again but I sensed something was wrong. I was five months along and I was Christmas shopping. Standing in line I began to hemorrhage. I was taken to the hospital, went through labor and gave birth to an unformed fetus. I was depressed, disappointed and discouraged.

We wanted a third child and I began praying that I would conceive again. I prayed and prayed to no avail. And then one day the doctor told me the good news, we would have another child. He said I would have to stay off my feet at the beginning months as much a possible. I was so frightened that I would miscarry again. I started having contractions at six months of pregnancy. This time I turned to God.

Learning about Jesus

I began reading the bible, I read about Jesus and the miracles that he preformed. I read that if we asked anything from the father in Jesus' name He would do it for us. One night I asked Jesus to come into my heart, take over my life and be Lord and savior and that is just what He did. I could feel His presence come into my room. I was changed, I was new. I belonged to Him. He would take me on a journey through life with Him by my side. Never leaving me; never forsaking me; always there.

The Birth of our Son

It was our anniversary and we planned to go out to dinner when the contractions started. Too early I thought, too early! Exactly six weeks too early.

I gave birth to a beautiful son, but he was too sick to be able to come to my room- He remained in an incubator away from the other newborns. He had no sucking ability and was born with a hemangioma on his right temple.

The prognosis was not a good one. The doctor said that if he lived he could be blind, epileptic, deaf, and have numerous other defects. I was devastated, picturing him spending the rest of his life in some home. The doctors said they would do tests that would take a week or two.

I took the phone off the hook; I wanted to speak to no one. I prayed, "Lord, how would I take care of a child like this?" Maybe it would be better if you took him home to heaven with you.

Our First Miracle

One night in the hospital there was a miserable storm. The thunder woke me; I started remembering Jesus' words " ask anything in my name." Lord I prayed, "You can do all things, You did the impossible. I ask you to give me my son for twenty one years." To this day I don't know why I asked for that specific number of years. At that time twenty-one years seemed like an eternity.

The First Sign

"Show me a sign that he will be healed" I said. What sign could I ask for at three in the morning, in a dark room with torrential rain outside? Then it came to me, I'll ask to see the sun, that would be quite impossible, I thought. Immediately a ray of sun came through my window and lit on flowers from my husband. They were on the bureau opposite the bed.

I knew He had granted my prayer. I was saying as I walked down the hall, "Jesus has healed my son." I went to the place were my son was- and I watched the hemangioma shrink down to nothing. Color began coming into his face. I said to the nurse "Look! Something has happened to my new child." Finally they called for my doctor to come. He was in the hospital delivering a baby. He came up to the nursery and tried to calm me down. He said to the nurse, "you see a change has taken place in this child, Try to feed him." For the first time in his life, he drank four ounces of milk. Before my very eyes I watched the amazing power of god at work, and my life would never ever be the same, nor would my sons.

The Healing Confirmed

That afternoon the pediatrician came to my room and said these exact words very calmly "Nature has reversed itself, in a miraculous way. I will circumcise your son and you can take him home." Positively amazing!- I thought.

We brought him home on Memorial Day. It was a calm, quiet peaceful day. I saw things differently then ever before. The sky, the trees, everything seemed brighter, more colorful than before. I felt like I was alive for the very first time. I was about to enter a different phase of my life, A life where Jesus would be Lord, healer, provider, protector, and most of all savior.

Another Sign From Above

My parents were with us the day we brought my son home and we were discussing his healing- Our two girls were on the front lawn playing. We were watching them through the bay window in our Levittown home. Our newborn was safe and sound in the crib in his room. Praise God! I said to my parents and husband, "I know I will be sharing this story for years to come. I would love the Lord to show me a sign that indeed it was Him that did this fabulous work in answering my prayers."

A Spinning Tree

We had a very large maple tree in front of our house near the sidewalk. As we watched through the window, in the stillness of this beautiful day, the tree began spinning until the roots began to emerge. Thinking we were about to have a tornado, my husband ran to get the girls. When he got outside the tree stood quietly as usual without a leaf even moving. We all witnessed this strange sight.

It was one of the most amazing sights I have ever seen and I remember it vividly, until this very day-God is amazing! Truly amazing! And He does very unusual things- our neighbor told us she had witnessed the amazing sight and took cover in her house. I explained the entire story to her and she believed it. I knew it was the Lord showing me " yes I heard you and answered, if you ask anything in my name, believing, I will do it for you."

Aside from my mom's ear being healed I had never heard of God healing anyone on the Earth except reading it in the Bible. It was all very very new to me and I needed to share this testimony with my priest, the one I confessed to, who was my confraternity teacher, the priest who married us. He was a wonderful kind man and I knew I could share anything with him.

Relating the Story to My Priest

Much to my surprise, He wasn't excited or happy for me. In fact, his only comment was that I should study Catholic theology in depth. It would help me understand what God was doing in my life. The studying did not help me at all. I had a true experience with the creator and I was going to search until I found Him. I stopped going to mass. I didn't want to know about religion. I wanted to know this powerful deity who stepped into my life and changed things forever.

As I am writing this, my search is not over. My prayer everyday is, " Lord reveal yourself to me, more and more everyday. Whom do you want me to help? Whom do you want me to encourage? Whom should

I pray for?" Ask him. He will put all kinds of people into your life who need you. Once you make yourself an open vessel He will open up a new world to you. A world of people in need. People who need you! You!

I felt bad leaving a church that I knew from childhood. Not only that but I took my girls out of religion classes, and I was responsible for that. I prayed for days " Lord show me the way" I knew He had a new plan for my life but as for now I was in the dark.

A New Direction

Then one day a young man came to lay carpet in our house. It was a very nasty day and I offered him lunch so he wouldn't have to go out. How we began speaking about God I do not know. This young man changed my direction. I was on a new path. The Lord sent him for sure. It was not a coincidence and I will never forget him.

Carpet Layers Story

He related this story to me. "I was a hopeless drug addict," he said. " I was in the hospital many times. I used all my veins. I even shot up in my nose" I was quite unfamiliar with these terms. He explained it to me in great detail. "All of my veins and skin were black with holes everywhere. My wife and my children left me. I was pathetic," he said. He was working with a man who each time he banged a nail said, "Praise the Lord." This irritated him so badly he asked to be moved to a different job. The Christian man told him to just stop at his church once and he would not bother him again. "There was no way I was ever going to put my foot in a church," The former drug addict said. One night he was driving home and stopped at a light. An audible voice said, " Go into the church on the corner." He thought it was his mind playing tricks on him, but, again he heard the voice. He parked the car and went in while there was a service going on. He sat quietly in the back. The pastor came down the aisle to him and said to follow him, He found his legs moving although he wanted to stay seated. At the altar the pastor laid his hands on him and said, "The next time you go to the hospital you will die. In Jesus' name be made whole." These were all foreign words to me but I was all ears.

He kept speaking and related the rest of the story to me. "My legs gave way and I found myself lying on the floor. I couldn't get up for a long while, and as I stood up I looked at my arms. They had brand new skin on them, that of a new baby. I never used drugs again. I'm united with my wife and family and the bible is my source of strength each day." The strange part, it wasn't even the Christian man's church, but God knows where you are- what you are in need of and how to get you were He wants you to go.

I asked him one question, where is the church? I had never heard a story of God's love like this. I was overwhelmed and so curious. There were churches that actually believed that God heals today? My curiosity led me to that church. Going to a different church to me raised catholic was not a good thing. Am I doing the will of God? I wasn't sure.

My Journey Began

I begged my mom to go with me. We went at night so no one would see us. It was very strange. People saying, "thank you Jesus" out loud- Men and women praising and worshipping the Lord! Where in the world were we? We were shocked! " Are these people normal?" I asked myself.

At the end of the service the pastor came down to us and introduced himself. I told him why I had come, about the drug addict and about my son's healing. He was actually overjoyed-Wow! I thought this man doesn't even know me and yet he believes my story. I found a place where they believe in healing and miracles. It took awhile for my husband to attend with me, but before long my family, including my very skeptical father came along as well.

It was a breath of fresh air. I wasn't alone; others also had the power of God work in their lives. It was all very new and we remained in that church for a few years enjoying the freedom of loving and praising God. I couldn't wait to get there every Sunday. I felt renewed. Alive! Clean! Forgiven! Accepted!

But I was still hungering for more of God. I knew He was a miracle worker and I wanted desperately to see his power at work- the Lord lead me to a different place- a place where I would grow spiritually and see the Lord do things that I would remember for the rest of my life.

A New Journey Begins

I read about a church in the newspaper where they were having an Acts 19 service. People brought in their drugs, cigarettes and things they were addicted to and burned them in a fire. It even mentioned Ouija boards that they were bringing into the church. I had been using a Ouija board never realizing that it was against God's word. I was curious so I went to this church to see what was happening.

Relics on the walls, wheelchairs, crutches and canes were hanging everywhere. It was a sight to see-Were these healings actually happening on Long Island?

We began attending regularly. My girls joined the choir and we stayed for many years. Every service was exciting and we watched the Lord's power at work week after week. My oldest daughter met her husband there. He is a marvelous man of God. They are still married today, some thirty years later.

Is Anything too Difficult

At the first service I attended there was a bald man sitting in front of me. The skin on the back of his head was lumpy and there was a large growth in the center. The pastor announced he would be praying for people with any kind of growth on their bodies. This man walked up to the altar and by the time he was back in his seat the tumor was almost gone. I was simply amazed! The God of the universe cares about us and hears and listens to our prayers? The more healings I saw the more my faith got stronger. I was in awe.

Cataracts Gone

I was in church on a Tuesday morning. A nun from the Catholic Church across the street came up for prayer. Cataracts came out of her eyes and stayed on her cheeks. People were cheering and praising the Lord. I'll never forget it

A woman had a massive tumor in her stomach. The buttons on her dress were stretched beyond capacity. After prayer the dress just hung and you could see how it had been stretched. The tumor was gone!

The pastor used to say he would pay for the ambulance to bring the sick into the church because he would not have to pay for them to return to the hospital- and what he said was true. Many did not return to the hospital. Jesus healed them. Every service was fabulous.

I remember a pastor coming to preach at our church. While he was praying for people oil oozed out of his hand and ran down his shirtsleeve. I was stunned! I started to believe the Lord could and would do anything and I still believe it to this day- I saw it with my own eyes.

We started believing God could do the impossible because God was doing the impossible. We saw His power at work. It was very new to us and to our children.

A Pup Raised From the Dead

I believe the Lord cares about every aspect of our lives. Everything that concerns us concerns Him, including animals I would soon find out. Could God actually answer prayers concerning an animal? The answer is yes-

I raised Poodle puppies and then Yorkshire Terrier puppies to try to add to our income. Our Yorkie gave birth to 3 pups, the last one was still born- very tiny. The girls insisted we pray for the pup and we did, but to no avail. My mom rubbed and rubbed it in a towel but nothing. We tried alcohol on its nose but nothing- after about ten minutes I gave up but my girls didn't "Jesus" they prayed, "You can heal anyone" and put their hands on the dead little one. We heard one peep and that was it and their prayers were answered- no need to say we never sold the puppy.

Teach Me to Give

One thing bothered me about attending churches other than Catholic churches. At Mass a dollar was a huge amount of money to give in the second collection I began to see 5, 10 and 20 dollar bills being given in collections. Being very new at all of this I began to wonder whether a monetary gain had anything to do with these services. In short I was skeptical. I asked the Lord to show me if He wanted me to give. I would give ten dollars in the offering and when I'd count my money I would never be minus the ten dollars. It happened several times so I tried something a little different one week. I gave ten dollars in one collection, two dollars at the next service and exactly sixty-seven cents at another. I thought I was clever, as I never had change in my money from teaching. The next morning there was a check. Yes! Twelve dollars and sixty-seven cents, from my doctor, from an insurance check overpaid three years prior. From that time on I knew the Lord wanted me to give and showed me that, as I did He would bless me monetarily and He has certainly done that through the years. Give! It will be given back to you. It's in His word and His word is always true-

A Blessing Back

There was a woman in one of the services. She was dressed poorly with holes in her shoes. I had a hundred dollar bill folded in my wallet saved to go to the flea market after church. In the service I heard in my spirit give her your hundred-dollar bill. After arguing a while I gave it to her and wondered, "Are you going to bless me Lord?" What a baby Christian I was. The very next day I had an appointment with the dentist. "Diane" he said, " I think there is a previous balance in your account" "Oh great!" I thought to myself. He returned from his office and said "Oh it's I who owe you. Your insurance overpaid one hundred dollars." Give and it shall be given back to you. What a great lesson to learn.

I'm not saying every time you give, a flying dove will have a hundred dollar bill in its mouth trying to bless you but I learned that it's priceless, the joy you receive from giving to others. God said it in His word, "If you do it to the least of my children, you do it unto me." That has stayed in my mind all these years- We are His hands extended on this earth. He has given us so much-His very life. Knowing Him makes you want to give to others in every way, and once you do, you will never stop. It will become part of your daily living.

Learning about Jesus and His wonderful ways is more rewarding and exciting than anything else on this earth. The more you learn the more you will be able to share with others who might be in the dark.

A Growth Disappears

I was very busy teaching piano which is still my profession today. I developed a growth at the side of my left eye. It became difficult to concentrate on music. I went to see a dermatologist who scheduled me for the removal of the growth.

I believe that the Lord heals; I've witnessed the impossible happen. The night before the surgery I said a simple prayer. Lord it will certainly increase my faith if I did not have to go for surgery. In the morning I went to brush my teeth, looked in the mirror and saw no growth. The Lord had, indeed removed it. I looked in my bed but never found it. Always share your testimonies with others it will encourage them. That miracle led to other people receiving miracles.

A student had a similar looking growth in her eye. I told her about the Lord's power and what He did for me. She revealed that even though she went to a Catholic school she didn't believe in God at all. We made an agreement, I would pray for that growth to leave in the name of Jesus, and if it did she would allow me to teach her what I learned from the Bible. The next week when she returned to her lesson the growth was gone. Praise His Name!

I began teaching her to pray in Jesus' name believing. The summer came and we did not see each other. In September I saw her again and she told me this story. She was riding in a car with two boys and another girl. The girls were in the back seat. The driver lost control of the car and went down an embankment on a very busy road by our home. The two boys were killed instantly. The car had turned over and she and her friend were trapped inside. The doors were jammed and she couldn't get out.

Using Jesus' Name

She remembered the prayer and prayed, " In Jesus' name be opened." She said the door flew open and landed at least ten feet from the car. She smelled smoke and was able to pull her friend out. Her friend was motionless. My student was studying to be a nurse. She could not find a heartbeat. She prayed for her, for life to come back into her body and her friend began to breathe again. They were both rushed to the hospital. They were both fine.

I write this so you who are reading will know that it is so important to share with others what God has done for you to increase their faith for their healing. Faith comes from hearing.

Another Eye Healed

A friend of mine in church had a cyst in her eye- I told her of my healing, and she replied, "If God can do that for you He could certainly can do it for me", and He did. When she returned the following week, the cyst was gone. Never keep what God has done in your life to yourself. Shout it from the roof tops "My God can do all things." He is no respecter of persons.

A Cyst Drained After Prayer

Just recently I was teaching a nurse who worked in the E.R. for many years. She said, "I will not be at my lesson next week. I have to have this cyst on my eye removed." After telling her what the Lord did for me she said, "It's been removed a few times before, but I believe. Can we pray?" We joined hands together at the piano and asked the Lord to remove the cyst.

This is her story, which I'm sure she will verify as the truth. "Diane," she said, "I was standing at the sink when I heard psst- it was the cyst. It began to drain until it was no more."

Since that day we prayed together for many things in her life and God has remained faithful in all things- Share your faith. Do Not be afraid. God will always give you the words to speak. Tell everyone, it doesn't matter what religious affiliation they have. People will listen. Maybe you will be the only one that will share with them the amazing power of God-. That's why it's so important. You might hold the key to their salvation. You might be the one who perks their interest in the God who created the universe.

Cataracts, what Cataracts??

Just recently my husband was diagnosed with the start of a cataract on his eye. We both went back for eye examinations. We pray everyday together and I spoke to the mountain for him. Cataract, I prayed in Jesus' name be cursed from the root.

After the examination my husband asked the doctor "what about the cataract?" "Cataract" he said, "what cataract?" "There is none"- My husband asked the nurse, " Do cataracts disappear?" "No," she said, "never."

Does prayer work? You better believe it does- He's our source, our creator, our healer, our everything. Learn to rely on Him, on His word- It's true! It worked for us and it will work for you.

The Lord Can Sell A Car

We had a yellow pinto that we wanted to sell. We tried and tried, for sale signs, advertisements, to no avail. One day we prayed at dinner that the Lord would bring a buyer. As we finished the prayer the door bell rang. A young man said, " Selling the pinto?" It was probably the fastest answer to any prayer we've ever prayed and yes, he bought the car.

Asking for a Baby

We were at a barbecue with my husbands' family. His two nieces were crying that they couldn't get pregnant. They both had miscarriages, " Have you ever prayed?" I asked them. " You can pray for that?" they replied? "Absolutely." The three of us joined hands and asked the Lord for a blessing. They each had a baby a day apart. He hears and answers prayers and He'll hear and answer yours! "You have not because, you asked not," He said.

My niece asked if I would pray for a friend of hers who had many invitro fertilizations because she could not become pregnant on her own. The last invitro was successful. She was pregnant with triplets. The doctors wanted her to abort one of the babies. She refused, she lost all three babies. I called her not knowing her at all trying to give her some comfort through this terrible ordeal. She was very distraught to say the least. When I began praying for her my prayer was that she would get pregnant by natural means. I knew this would be impossible and that God would get all the glory. Yes, it happened and now she has a beautiful baby girl. I believe in the power of prayer-

I believe Jesus has given us the authority over all things on this earth. Nothing's impossible, it is not only healing that the Lord is interested in. It's in every aspect of your life.

A Beautiful Boy

I teach two wonderful children, a boy ten years old and an adorable five-year-old little girl. Their mother informed me that after three miscarriages she was pregnant again. She's a Christian woman and asked me to pray that she would not loose this baby. I don't think she fully understood the amazing power of God. I began praying each day "Fetus be strong, be healthy in Jesus' name." She began praying that way as well. Each week that I saw her she said the child in her womb was thriving.

This past summer she gave birth to a healthy baby boy. She brought him in last week. What a wonderful example of answered prayer. His smiling face encouraged my faith to believe no matter what the situation. No matter how bleak it looks He can step in and change the outcome.

A New Home

After living ten years in our home in Levittown we wanted to upgrade. We had a large expanded ranch. Every time I wanted to add a room I borrowed the money from my mother-in-law and paid her back little by little. We had seven rooms on one level. Very difficult to sell the real estate broker informed us. We prayed together for the Lord to bring us a buyer. The very next day a woman came to see our house. She had a special needs son who needed all the rooms on one floor because of the difficulty he had in walking. We sold the house immediately. I didn't realize God was in the real estate business, but I figured if He could sell my house He could find me the new house as well and that He did.

In my younger days I used to go to people's houses to teach piano. I was praying for a specific house, one where I could teach and not bother my neighbors with cars driving to and from lessons.

While I was giving a lesson in Bethpage, my student's mother asked me if perhaps I was looking for a house. She explained the house on the corner across the street from a children's playground was for sale, only through a lawyer that she knew personally. What a find. We secured a G.I. Mortgage. It was perfect. The cars could park and bother no one. It would be our new home, the one we still live in today. God is a superior house hunter. Do you believe He can do anything? He can!

My Daughter's House

When my oldest daughter and my future son-in-law were looking for a house they also prayed for the Lord to bring them the right one. They were struggling financially. Their funds were limited.

I was going to pick up my younger daughter from school one day. There was a detour because they were working on sewers in our town and alot of roads were impassable.

As I was driving I was praying please Lord find them a house like you found mine. They both love you so much. I added, it would be so beneficial if they did not have to pay real estate fees.

I now was rather lost. I heard an inner voice say make a right turn. I did turn right and there on the right side of the road was an adorable house with a tiny for sale sign in the window. The owner was coming home from work and said he would be glad to show them the house.

The price was out of their range. They prayed and made him an offer. I had no faith that he would accept it and he didn't. My children did not waiver and several weeks later he called and accepted their offer. It was the first of several homes they would buy. My son-in-law as long as I have known him has always given God all the glory. He has put him first and God has blessed abundantly. He is a marvelous born again, lawyer now and does alot of wonderful work for the Lord. Both my husband and I are very proud of the man he has become.

He Did It Again

Years later one of my students mothers, was trying to sell her house. It had been on the market for over a year and they were now paying for two homes. I told her how the Lord sold my house in Levittown bringing the exact buyer. She asked me to pray. We believed God and within one week her house sold for more than she asked for originally.

The extra ten thousand dollars she gave to her church. He knows everything- just ask.

My nephew and niece moved south and gave an offer on a lovely home with six acres of property. They would not accept their offer for weeks. My nephew called me and asked me to pray – I believe that God is interested in every part of our lives. That very next morning they called him to tell him the house was theirs. Does he listen and answer? He certainly does. He will do more than you can think or imagine.

Our First Grandchild

My daughter was pregnant with her first child. We were all ecstatic- a new baby in our family. How awesome!

Two months prior to my daughters due date she went into premature labor. My daughter and son-in-law had dedicated the baby to the Lord the moment she suspected that she was pregnant.

The doctor told Dan, my son in law, that although Cindy, my daughter, was fine the baby had many problems. I was not allowed in to see our new granddaughter so I will quote my son-in-law.

"When I went into the intensive care nursery I saw the most horrible sight I have ever seen – my baby girl lying on a miniature operating table with six tubes running to and from various parts of her body; her eyes blindfolded under the intensive lights, her head held tightly between a special vice, and the respirator machine pumping 100% oxygen into her inflating and deflating her like a balloon. I was told my baby was born without lungs and had small alveoli instead. Therefore she cannot breathe and needed a life support system to supply her with oxygen. She also had a hole (ductus) in her heart which had not closed, non functional kidneys and liver, and a fever coupled with an infection." My son-in-law believed in God. He laid his fingers on his baby's forehead and prayed that God would heal his child. Then he announced that the baby was going to be OK in front of at least six doctors.

My daughter and son-in-law were informed that the oxygen level had been lowered from 100% to 60% then two days later to 30% and then to 21%- The miracle was taking place.

The doctor said she had never seen anything like it before and acknowledged that a higher power had certainly intervened. That Indian doctor later became a Christian because of her healing-

A Straight Foot

When my granddaughter was several months old she was going to get fitted for a brace on her leg as it was turning outward instead of the way it should be normally.

We were in church on a Tuesday morning. There was a child on the altar being prayed for with a clubfoot. As we were praying for this child I heard something like a sound of light bones cracking. My granddaughter straightened out her foot and it has been perfect since that day.

She is now a talented woman who is a lawyer, can sing beautifully, teaches piano, and rides horses. She is such a blessing to us and we are so very grateful to God for what He has done in our lives.

A Leaking Valve

One day I took my son to the doctor because of a sore throat. The doctor put the stethoscope to Ricky's chest and began frowning. He moved it to another spot and listened again and then to another. His face looked grave and concerned. He called his associate in and they both agreed. There was an abnormality in his heartbeat that had the potential of being very serious. We were to go to a pediatric cardiologist immediately and have him undergo more extensive tests to determine what the problem was.

Within the week we found out that there was a leak in the valve in one of the chambers of his heart. Until it could be determined if the condition was worsening or remaining constant, nothing could be done. We had to keep checking him regularly to see what was happening. We made sure we made every appointment the doctors wanted. We began praying to the Lord for another miracle to take place in his life. We were expecting something good to happen. We serve such an awesome God.

The doctor wanted to take some cardiac x-rays to put in the permanent record file of Rick's condition. We took him in for the test and waited and prayed. "Lord by your stripes he was healed" In the examination room we were told, " When I examined your son before, the heart valve defect was quite pronounced. The reason I examined him today in such lengthy detail is- quite simply I was not able to find it at all." The doctor could not give us a medical explanation for what had happened.

It wasn't necessary! Jesus is our explanation of all things, which are impossible. I rest in Him knowing. He hears and answers.

Why am I crying?

We went to Lee Massachusetts one fall- Going up we watched the beautiful change of colors on the trees. They were completing a roof replacement at the inn we were supposed to stay at, so we stayed at another inn run by the same owner. It was lovely.

In the living room was a piano. Before dinner I began playing some of the music the Lord gave me. I've written several songs for Him. This woman came over to me and asked me " why am I crying when you play?" When we spoke together she revealed that she was a pastor's wife. He was unfaithful to her and she was contemplating leaving him. She said that weekend she asked the Lord to give her a sign that she should stay with him. She said that song I wrote "We are His children," touched her spirit and she was going to return home and give him another chance- The Lord will even use music to soften hearts. I was so thrilled that He used me.

A Fall From a Roof

When I first graduated from music college I began working at a place called the American Conservatory of Music. One of the men who taught there was an organist and played at various restaurants and clubs. I would later be his children's music teacher. His wife was the secretary at the conservatory.

One day he had a terrible accident. He fell off a roof and severely injured his back. He had to stop working, use a walker and was in a very depressed state.

I pleaded with him to come to church because I was witnessing so many healings; He wanted no part of it. He simply did not believe that God was real and was a healer. I gave up trying to convince him to come. Sometimes you get weary from trying.

Then one evening his wife called and said he was in such pain that he wanted to commit suicide. He asked to go to church.

It was a Tuesday morning service; she took her children out of school to bring them. In the morning she called to say all the tires on her car were flat. I replied, "Get there however you can. He must be in store for a miracle." A hunched over man on a walker-straightened up-threw aside the walker and was miraculously healed in the name of Jesus and he is still healed to this day.

Because of Plants

I was teaching a woman who worked in a nursery for plants. Every time she came in for a lesson she would say to me " Something is different about you." She was a lovely woman, a Jewish lady and I did not want to take the time from her lesson to tell her all that had happened to me.

Then an ice storm hit over our area. We lost all power and we took refuge in our den with the fireplace roaring. Several days we lived like that. The milk actually froze on our kitchen table. We decided to move to my brother's house that did have heat and light. I am a plant lover and I felt so bad that all my plants would die. Before we left I actually did pray that my plants would survive.

We kept checking on the house to see if everything was all right. After looking in the house one day I proceeded to go to the bank to cash some checks. When I stopped at the stop sign, the same voice I heard many times said, "go back to the house." I thought that was strange since I was just there and continued to drive. When I heard it the second time I turned around. When I got into the den I heard the sound of rushing water. A pipe had burst and now the water was pouring out of the den ceiling. If I had continued driving to the bank our house would have been destroyed.

God Protects Plants

After a period of at least two weeks we moved back into our house. Every plant was still in bloom, not one was frozen. It taught me that you could pray for anything. God is merciful. He hears and he cares about everything that we care about.

When the woman came back and I told her about all the plants surviving. She asked if she could meet me for lunch. I kiddingly said "wherever I go the Lord goes with me."

Three For Lunch

We met at a Japanese restaurant, It was early for lunch and it was quite empty. The host took us to the table and said, "three of you?" I said promptly "no two of us." He sat us at one of those long tables; He put three place settings down and walked away. Now she said to me "is there anyone else with us?" I laughed and said, " of course not." We just sat there waiting. The waiter came and said, " Has the gentleman left?" I said "yes" and he began waiting on us. I told this woman the many things the Lord had done in my life. She asked to go to church with me. I explained that there was a large large cross on the altar but she still wanted to go. Was the Lord or and angel with us- I don't know-

She loved church immediately; it really surprised me. She was raised as a Jewish woman her whole life.

Cancer Healed

Soon after her son who was almost thirteen had a large swelling in his side. They thought it was from a hockey accident. After more examinations they sent him to our local hospital. The diagnosis was grim. A large cancerous tumor in his side. His mom asked if our pastor would go and pray for him. Of course he went. The doctors decided to send him to Sloan-Kettering to remove the tumor. It would be a long operation as the tumor had wrapped itself around various organs. I spoke to his mom each day; she was positively convinced that God had healed him. My faith for the situation was not strong at all. I kept trying to explain to her that all people that are prayed for are not immediately healed. God's timing, I explained, is not our timing. I kind of felt sorry to be honest that I ever started the whole thing. She, however, would not be moved. He was healed and that was that!

When the operation would take place they told her to get a bed in his room because the operation would be twelve to fourteen hours. She replied, " There will be no need for a bed or an operation." God honored her faith. When they opened him up to remove the tumor there was no tumor. God had certainly performed a marvelous miracle. How awesome He is!

A Swollen Vein

One day during a routine examination my husband was informed that they found a mass in his chest near his heart. Needless to say we were both very upset. We prayed and believed. After many sonograms and tests they gave us the results. They said they didn't understand but they couldn't find the mass. It must have been a swollen vein. The Lord did it again. He is our source, our strength, and our protection.

Mom Moved In

My mom moved in with us when my father became ill. She was always my best friend, always supportive; I was thrilled to have her with us. She probably had more faith then anyone I know. A true believer. As I think about her now, I picture her in the back seat of our car- praying always praying. She prayed in polish, in English, said the rosary, constantly in prayer.

Flu Bows it Knees

The first healing I remember after she moved in with us was one Sunday she had a very bad flu. My dad was in the hospital and she wanted to go but was immobile in bed.

I went into her room and prayed for her in Jesus' name. She got up saying "I'm healed," got dressed and went to the hospital. I think that day I fully realized how powerful the name of Jesus is, and to think He gave us His name to use. Amazingly, the God of the entire universe hears our requests and sometimes like in this case, heals immediately.

The Gift of Knowledge

My mom started getting chest pains, the doctor said these words "your mother's cardiogram is whacko!" Then he explained in medical terms what was wrong. Her heart was enlarged and it wasn't beating properly. He said he would be afraid to do any operation at her age, for fear of causing a stroke.

My mom had pain when she walked and literally went around the house on her backside all the while saying, "I'm healed in Jesus' name."

I replied, "You don't seem as if you're healed." "Nonsense" she said, "I'm healed," I kept praying and praying for her but saw no physical change.

One evening I begged her to go to church with me. I just felt the Lord urging us to go. It was a Wednesday night service, which I rarely attended. After some persuading she decided to go-with great difficulty. It was crowded as usual; we sat in the balcony in the very back of the church.

Our pastor was out of town and a visiting pastor was ministering. He was in the very front of the church, which was quite a distance. In the middle of the sermon he turned toward the back and said, "Stella, God is going to give you a new heart. You will be able to walk and run again." I was crying uncontrollably as I had never told anyone anything was wrong with my mom. The power of God was so strong that she could not stand. She fell out in the spirit and lay there for quite awhile. This minister said "whoever touches this women will be healed as well." Many people came and touched her and could not stand. It was a sight to see that's for sure. The power of God!

When she got off the floor she said, "Diane, I feel marvelous! Jesus has touched me!" From then on she walked a few miles every-day giving glory to God. She was a walking miracle until the day the Lord took her home to heaven, which was probably twenty years after this healing. By the way the doctor was totally amazed. He could not believe the change in the cardiogram. It was astounding. My faith and my mom's faith grew and grew.

Healing On Teeth

One day we were in church and the pastor said there was a visiting pastor coming Friday night. There was going to be a communion service and for some reason there were many healings on teeth. This did not sit well with my husband or me. I didn't believe that God was interested in our teeth, thinking God was much too busy to take interest in someone's molars. It sounded absurd to me and both my husband and I decided we definitely would not go. My son, however, said to his grandmother, "I believe God can do anything and I will take you." So off they went.

Prior to this our granddaughter who was about five years old came to our house often. She would ask to see her grandmother's teeth. My mom would say "do not eat candy and your teeth will not look like this."

Black Teeth

Several times this took place and finally I said, " Mom let me see your teeth." There were a lot of dark fillings but nothing too unusual for her age. Little did I know that God was preparing me for what was going to take place- I would never have believed it if I hadn't seen them before. Mom wasn't too fond of the dentist to say the least. She also had two small holes in her eyetooth. I kept urging her to go and have them fixed but it never happened.

The day my son and my mom went to that service I said, "Mom if God works on teeth show him the holes while you're there and maybe He will fix them for you." Needless to say she didn't find it amusing.

My son and mom went off to church that night. My husband and I went out to dinner, not interested in any strange thing God might do in your mouth.

Twelve Gold Teeth

This is the story my mother related to us about that night. "I went and took communion and when I sat back down in my seat a lady said to me "I have a silver filling where I did not have it before," my mom said, " I'm going back for a double portion," and went for communion again. When she sat down she took out a mirror to see whether God might have done something for her. To her amazement twelve teeth in the bottom of her mouth were filled with gold.

She came home and knocked on our bedroom door, "Tony," she said, " I want you to see something," He said " mom its after eleven. Show me in the morning." "No!" she cried, " you must see it now." When we saw what God had done we were baffled! Each tooth had a cross-etched in it and they were all filled with gold. I for one would never be the same. That miracle took me through the worst time of my life. I knew it was strange but I never believed you walk on streets of gold in heaven. It sounded too un-imaginable to me. Now it seems possible, if God could fill someone's teeth with gold- He could do anything! As you read this believe him for anything. He can do it!

Don't give up! Never give up! Never! We spent the weekend praising God- How awesome!

That Saturday night friends of ours came over- We were going out to dinner. He happened to be an oral surgeon. My mom was so excited to show him what had happened. When he looked in her mouth he said, "Stella, why would you pay so much money for gold fillings?" and then added " Wow! What amazing bridge work! I've never seen anything like it!" My mom never had any bridgework done! She said to him " Jesus did it!" Of course he really could not understand that and we certainly couldn't explain it to him. And remember those two holes in her eyetooth? They were filled with two gold hearts.

I thought it was a sign from God for our family and those gold fillings would disappear, but no, they were there until the day the Lord took her home to walk on those streets of gold. I don't know why God gave her such an unusual miracle I just know it made a profound impact on my life, and I just knew that this life is not it. Life is not over when it's over on this earth. We have a father in heaven that has prepared a marvelous place for us. Walking on streets on gold- and living in mansions. Yes it's in his word.

Tumor Disappears

Soon after I had two sisters come in for piano lessons. They seemed very upset. Their mom had to be operated on for a tumor on her ovary the next day. I tried to comfort them telling them what an awesome God He is. He would watch over their mom.

That night I telephoned their mother at the hospital. I really did not know her personally but I felt the Lord prompting me to call her and pray for her. She was very receptive praying with me for her healing.

I couldn't fall asleep and continued to pray into the night. The next morning the telephone rang. It was she calling. I said " are you going in for surgery now?" "Surgery?" she said. "I'm home." Then she explained the doctor came in and said for some reason he could not fall asleep the night before and before doing surgery he wanted to do another sonogram. The tumor shrunk ninety-seven percent. He sent her home. I went to her home that morning with a Bible in my hand, encouraging her to learn more about the awesome God who shrunk that tumor.

I started to realize how very powerful prayer is and how important it is for us to pray for those in need.

Knowing His Voice

I began recognizing his voice in my spirit " my sheep will know my voice" He said.

I was going to take my car to be serviced when I got off the expressway. I needed to get over to the left but there was so much traffic I decided to go into a street where there was a red light. That way I would be able to cross over the busy highway and go right into the dealership. The light was green and I proceeded to go. A voice said, "Stop now" I knew this voice and I did stop before crossing the thoroughfare. A huge truck carrying maybe six or seven cars ran through the red light speeding- As I tried to catch my breath I realized I would have been right in his path. It would have been some collision for sure. That voice saved my life. The precious voice of the Lord. How awesome! I learned to love that still small voice. Listen always listen!

Warnings

One night I had a dream. In the dream I was parked in a parking lot of a store near us that sold only produce. A red car pulled up, lost control and smashed into my car where I was parked. I was still in the car. Unusual dream I thought.

Two days later I stopped at a vegetable stand. As I was going into the store I saw the red car driving into the lot. I re-entered my car and moved it to the back. I heard a great commotion. The red car crashed into the market sending vegetables and fruit everywhere. If I had stayed in the car I would have been hit. I believe the Lord will warn you of certain things even if it is in a dream. Heed the warning!

A Heavenly Dream

One night, the night before Easter I dreamt the Lord took me up a stairway that seemed like it never ended. I had pajamas on and I was barefooted. When we got to the top he said, "Take my hand." We started descending ever so slowly in the air. Through my toes I could see a city shining. I had never seen anything so bright. Many houses were made out of glass and the streets were gold. He said to me "this is as far as you can go." I found myself in bed but I could still see the city. It seemed as if I was awake but still in that dream for a few minutes.

We will someday be walking on those streets of gold I thought and then finally fully awake I began praising and worshipping Him shouting "He is risen! He is real" Needless to say I woke the whole house up but it was a marvelous experience which I will never forget. I saw that city in heaven- He has prepared a place for us.

We're Protected

Just recently I had a very real dream. It was July as it is now. I walked out on my deck and I saw what looked like a ball of fire come down from the sky. It hit the house next to me and the shattered wood was flying all over. It was destroyed! Then in my side yard an enormous angel came down. He had golden hair and a shield and a sword drawn. Then another angel appeared a little higher than the first. He looked the same. Then one more angel came a little higher. They all stood there with their swords drawn. I stood there with my mouth open; and suddenly it began snowing. Another ball of fire came toward my house and it landed on the umbrella and just stayed there. Whether or not this was a warning I do not know. But I do know that my Lord said He would protect us and I have no fear of anything that's coming on this earth. He's returning soon, I know all the signs and they are happening everyday. Are you ready? If you know Him you are children of the light.

Witnessing On An Operating Table

In a routine examination my doctor discovered a lump in my breast. Explaining it was nothing- I did not have it out- I prayed many times for a healing but it never happened. When the doctor's son took over the practice and discovered the lump he insisted I go to a breast surgeon- She tried to aspirate it to no avail. Surgery was necessary- When I got into the operating room I lay on the table for what seemed like an eternity. No nurse, no doctor, no anything- just me so I started to pray. When the nurse came in I said to her, "Thank goodness I'm a praying women otherwise I would been a wreck lying here." The nurse said, "I used to pray but not anymore." I replied, "Do you believe in miracles?" she said "no." I began telling her about my mom's teeth. Now the anesthetist came in and the nurse said " Do not touch her before she finishes telling me the rest of the story." Now the breast surgeon came in and they all hovered around me until I finished telling them how God filled my mom's mouth with gold- I do not know what became of the nurse but I do know I was there for that purpose. After surgery I came to my room, I actually felt refreshed. My doctor came in "How are you doing?" "I want to go home" I replied. " I'll be back in forty- five minutes. If you can walk a straight line, I'll discharge you." I was operated on at nine thirty and at eleven thirty I went to lunch with my husband." Don't worry" she said " you can bet you'll feel those stitches." I went home expecting to cancel lessons because of pain. I never even felt a twinge. He never ceases to amaze me. He will use you even on an operating table.

A Heart Problem

I went for a pre-op testing before removing this lump in my chest. I found a message on my answering machine. My cardiogram did not come out well. I needed to see a cardiologist before surgery would be allowed. I took several tests. The results were not great. There were three doctors. The first doctor said he thought it was very serious. The second doctor said the same thing. The third doctor said it might not be so terrible. I said, "I'll go along with the third doctor." They found I had a mitral valve prolapse. I had to be on medication especially when going to a dentist. I had to be on antibiotics but that was a better prognosis than was thought.

Every time I prayed while playing piano on the altar I asked God for a healing and then one time I had to take an echo cardiogram. They could not find the mitral valve prolapse. No more antibiotics- I was free-

Get Dressed And Go Home

One time I was scheduled for a procedure called cryosurgery where they freeze the cervix. I had many problems since the birth of my oldest daughter. She was a very large baby and after two days of labor my cervix was torn open when she was born. This time the doctor needed special equipment for the procedure. The night before I was in church, I went up for prayer and the lord touched me because when I went to have it done the doctor examined me and said, " I don't know what happened but everything looks fine." I thankfully put on my clothes and hurried home. I'm truly blessed.

I believe sometimes we go through different things and sometimes He heals us but what I've learned is He is always with us one way or another. He never leaves us, never! I also believe He is in absolute control of all things including the weather.

Be Calm

Our family rented a beautiful home on the water at the outer banks in North Carolina for a week in the summer. As we were driving the last part of our trip we heard on the radio of a hurricane headed toward the coast of North Carolina. That is not good as there is only one road that leads you in and out of the towns on the outer banks and when they say you must evacuate it is bumper to bumper for hours and hours. When we arrived the wind was already very strong. I told everyone don't unpack for I believe we were going to be leaving shortly. My son-in-law who is definitely a man of faith said, " Who believes that this hurricane will not hit us?" Well from all the reports and from what I could see I did not have such a faith because by this time the winds were very strong.

My son-in-law said "lets go food shopping we will be here for a week." That seemed absurd to me considering the situation. His parents, my son-in-law and I prayed for the hurricane to blow out to sea and we set out for the food market. Not smart I thought.

I began preparing dinner listening to very discouraging reports on the radio. As we were sitting down to dinner looking out at a raging ocean we thanked God again for a wonderful vacation. Then another report came- For some unknown reason the hurricane was turning away from the outer banks. We were all ecstatic, praising and worshipping the creator. All week the winds were very powerful- and the children really couldn't swim, but I learned a marvelous lesson. Do not limit the God that made the ocean and the sea. He can calm them.

He's In Control

When my son-in-law and daughter became engaged I planned an engagement party in our yard. About fifty people were going to attend, the forecast for that day was heavy rain, and there was a tornado in the next town. We prayed and prayed for the Lord to hold back the rain. After all He was the one who calmed the sea so He has control over the weather- The skies were black when people started to come- the caterers still set up chafing dishes. People from Brooklyn said they were driving through very inclement weather. Three blocks from our home it was pouring. The sky stayed black over our house- and I will never forget getting into bed that night thanking God. The rain came down in buckets and continued through the night. He is concerned with every aspect of our lives and He said, " You have not because you ask not." Ask! He cares about everything-

No Room At The Inn

As I am writing these different incidents one comes to mind where the Lord showed that He was with us, watching over us. Everything that happened wasn't always earth shattering but I knew He was with us- On one vacation we were coming back from Canada- We were a day early arriving in Booth Bay Harbor, Maine. The tall ships were in the harbor and we were in the midst of traffic, we were trying to get into town. The bed and breakfast we were to stay in was not available because of our early arrival- Literally no place to stay. My son was so upset- "we'll have to leave." he said "no," I said, "We have to pray." "You really think Mom, with all these crowds of people that we are going to get a room?" he replied. I knew this was an easy one for the Lord so I picked the beautiful inn directly on the water and went into the office. When I asked for a place to stay, the receptionist laughed saying we've been booked for this day for the last eight months. I thanked her and as I was about to leave, the telephone rang. "Wait one minute "she said and then explained, "Someone cancelled a suite directly on the water." We had an amazing view of all the tall ships. His timing is always perfect! He intervened many times when we were traveling. What a view! Only the best for God's children-

Suitcases Lines Up

My husband and I were flying to Venice to take a cruise down to the Greek islands with friends. We got to the airport and waited and waited. They explained to us that the crew was held up in traffic. That seemed a little odd to us but we boarded the plane and flew to Frankfurt, Germany. There we were to get our connecting flight to Venice. However, we were late and that flight left without us and about twelve other people. They really had no idea what to do with us. There were no other planes to Venice that day so they decided to fly us to Milan and then bus us to Venice. First they took us to their restaurant to feed us lunch. The others were all upset because they said they would never have their luggage. I replied "We will have our luggage," I will pray and the Lord will take care of it- I already knew that He was concerned with every aspect of our life not only the physical. Needless to say the other people with us avoided me like the plague. Somehow when Jesus enters the conversation people tend to flee.

The airport personnel drove us out to a large open field where guards with weapons were patrolling. Trucks with luggage on them came and they began throwing the luggage over this field and in the background was the plane. People were frantically searching for their belongings strewn all over.

There in the midst of all the chaos was our luggage standing in order one, two, three-the fourth one missing. As if He knew exactly where it belonged a man lifted the last one out of the truck and placed it orderly, behind the others. They took them in the plane and we boarded. Out the window I watched everyone still searching. I wanted to shout to them see, you should have asked the Lord but I quietly thanked Him for caring about us. My husband exclaimed " if I wasn't a believer I would have become one today-"

Free Breakfast

I learned wherever you go He is with you, watching over you, using you. We were in a place called Rocca De Poppa, the highest elevated town outside of Rome. We stayed at a lovely hotel. A young man from England took care of our needs and we began talking before we went to dinner. The conversation somehow turned to God and he said "I do not pray to God anymore, He does not love me, He disowned me." He explained that he was a Jesuit priest and left the priesthood. We spoke for quite a while and I told him there was no way God forsook him. He said in His word I will never leave you or forsake you- Those words are true today. It doesn't matter the situation, He'll always be there and He will take you back with open arms as He did the prodigal son. I told him to pray and ask Him to renew His relationship to the father and son. He said, "If He does, everything is on me including your breakfast."

In the morning he was waiting for us with a big smile. He said, " It worked! Breakfast is waiting." Before we left we hugged and hugged. I wrote to him for years and years. Never hold back, tell everyone how forgiving and loving the Lord is. Use these two words "use me" and watch what the Lord will do in your life.

A New Dining Room

Is He concerned with everything? Yes, every detail of your life. I was at a service in our church. The pastor said, "is there anything you desire today? Why not enjoy it while you're still alive." I came home and sat on my step. I tried hard to think of something I wanted but I couldn't. Then it dawned on me I always wanted an antique looking dining room set. It certainly wasn't a necessity just something I would have liked. I put an ad in the newspaper and the first person that came in bought my old set even though it was not in good condition.

The Hunt Began

I began going to various stores asking the salesman if they had a set like I was explaining. Store after store, no dark antique looking set. Then one day I stopped at a furniture store on 110- a busy highway not too far from our house. The salesman's hand was wrapped in a bandage. I asked him what was wrong. He had to go for surgery the next day he explained. I explained what I was looking for and he lead me to it in the back of the store. I loved it and gave him a deposit. Before I left I asked if I could pray for his hand. " oh yes," he said." I wish you would." Two days later he called saying I will deliver your set for free and I will drop the price three hundred and fifty dollars. I was elated. He was healed and cancelled surgery. Not saying I ever would want a reward for praying for people but when God gives me a blessing I'm certainly willing to say " thank you Lord. Praise your holy name!"

Now one week later I took a friend of mine to the store. She was looking for a piece of furniture. The store was completely empty and locked up – No sign on the door, just closed- Was it only there for me? I'll never know!

Upgraded Car

When I first started to really know Jesus, we went to Europe with our cousins and we drove through five countries. We rented an opal Escuner for the trip never realizing that an opal Escuner is the size of a refrigerator. When we saw it we laughed- " isn't there any other car you can give us?" I pleaded. We were in Frankfort Germany without any knowledge of the language- the man was quite emphatic, "no, there is no other car available," By this time I realized that God really does hear and answer prayer. I told my cousins I was going to pray for a different car. Of course they thought I had a screw loose- My prayer was, "Lord you can do anything- Could you find us a different car?" when I went back to the man He said " Let me see what I might be able to do." Out came a new red Mercedes. They'll be no extra charge- Everyone including me- was stunned- What a mighty God- we have not because we ask not. What a fantastic scripture.

A Bone Disappears

I had an operation on my nose some years back. I had a deviated septum and while that was being taken care of I had my nose made smaller which was my hearts desire for many years. After the operation a small bone protruded out of the left side of my nose. The doctor said he would operate on it again and fix the situation. We were scheduled to go on a trip to the Canadian Rockies. He said it could wait so we left for Seattle to meet a tour. There were about thirty people who were going to travel with us. They asked everyone when they wanted to have dinner. My husband and I always ate late and opted for the latest time. So did another couple from Brooklyn. We hit it off immediately and spent the whole trip with them.

There was also a wonderful man traveling with his sister. I soon learned he was a priest in layman's clothes. He wasn't at all upset with me that I had left the Catholic Church. We only were excited because we shared a love- the love of the Lord- Each day when the weather looked terrible we would pray. The sun would come out and we'd rejoice that God heard our prayer- Soon others would ask us to pray when threatening clouds would appear.

We were staying one day at a gorgeous hotel in Jasper. The couple we had dinner with each night very quickly became our friends. He was extremely funny and she was delightful, the head of physical education in N.Y.C. We discussed many things. I told them of many experiences with God-

She expressed an interest to have a nose operation. I showed her my protruding bone and told how all nose operations don't always come out perfectly. So she noticed the bone when I had called her attention to it.

River Rafting

The next day the four of us decided to go white water rafting. I had never done such a thing because I can't swim, and I am deathly afraid of the water. So was my new friend, but both of us agreed not to chicken out. When the priest heard I was going he said "I will have to pray for your protection before you go."- I said "Father we are leaving at six thirty in the morning." He said, "I'll be there." He came down to the bus we were leaving on in his bathrobe and he kind of shook his hand over my face and prayed a quick prayer. I thought it a little odd to get up so early for such an unusual prayer, but I thanked him and off we went. Never refuse a prayer.

We weren't too far from the hotel and we had beautiful weather and a real fun time. However, they were so worried about us because the storm they were experiencing at the hotel was so severe that a man was hit by lightening and killed. When I heard about it I was so happy about the priest's prayer.

That night our friends and we went to the top floor of the hotel to have dinner. The view was spectacular. As we were eating I touched the side of my nose which was a habit feeling that protrusion. This time there was no bone. My left side of my nose was perfectly smooth. It overwhelmed me and I started to cry. "I didn't even ask God to heal me this time," I said. Our friends were amazed, I excused myself and went out to an outside patio. I started praising God and a rainbow, the most vibrant one I've seen, crossed right over my head- Could it be I got a healing when the priest prayed that unusual prayer waving his hand in my face and nose?

A Priest With A Mission

The next day the priest was sitting down by the water reading his bible. I went down and told him the story. He began to cry and said, "Diane, I came on this trip asking the Lord for guidance. I'm a chaplain at a hospital and I'm so tired of giving people last rites. I wanted to be able to pray for them and have them live and not die. You are that answer to my prayer. I will go back renewed with a purpose.

We wrote to each other for years. Telling each other of the wonders of the Lord. This past Christmas a card came back. My dear friend had gone home to be with the Lord. I know He's walking on those streets of gold and I will certainly see him again. There are no coincidences with God. They are his handiworks.

Yes I still speak to the friends we met. They live in New Jersey, every friend we meet is important to us. We stay in touch with them.

My operation was cancelled. My doctor was baffled. Oh the wonderful pleasures of serving the Lord. The unexpected things that He does for us. I still am in awe of His marvelous ways. A friend, a savior, a healer, a provider, a protector, He's everything, I am so thankful that He chose me.

Providing Shelter

While traveling in France with friends we came to a place called Gorda, a town on a steep hill with nothing but rocks everywhere. You had to park on the top of the hill- A car couldn't go down the winding roads of the town- It was just the most unusual place I've ever seen in all my travels. We had no place to stay and it was already dusk. We began walking down to see if there might be a pension or a small hotel somewhere, but there was nothing- All you saw everywhere were rocks- I began to pray- Lord please find us a place to stay.

When we returned to our car there was a flyer on our window- Need a place to stay? In English no less with directions- We followed a road for miles seeing nothing anywhere but rocks and rocks and then there it was a beautiful Inn- Of course there were two rooms available- We had dinner outside- the couple cooked it for us- It didn't seem real- like a dream. My husband said as we left " Don't look back; it will have disappeared." I guess the Lord is in the travel business as well.

A Trip To A Villa

My brother rented a beautiful villa in Jamaica one winter. It was the February recess and all our families were going for a restful vacation. The day we were to leave we had a major snowstorm and all the airports were closed down. I called Air Jamaica to see if we could possibly go the next day. "Impossible," she replied. The next plane available would be four days later. I put the phone down and saw the children's faces so distraught. They said "Lets pray and ask the Lord to get us on that plane tomorrow, please call back." They begged. I called and asked to speak to a supervisor. The woman said I would have to be willing to wait at least a half hour to speak to one.

When she finally got on the telephone I explained our dilemma. Our tickets are for today and because of the snow storm the airport is closed. I explained how our children and I prayed. She said, "oh you're a praying woman? Let me put your names in the computer and see what happens." She came back and said, "Your tickets are in the computer for tomorrows flight. Check them." We did but the tickets were not for the next days flight. She told us all to come to the airport the next day and say nothing.

I silently prayed all the way to the airport. The snow piled high on either side of the road. When we arrived people were actually fighting trying to board with yesterday's tickets. It was bedlam.

The women took the tickets from sixteen of us. She looked straight at the wrong date and motioned us through! I almost fainted. How was this possible? It wasn't!

When we were seated comfortably an officer came on the plane and made several people get off who had the tickets from the day before. He never bothered us and we were on our way thanks to our heavenly father, sixteen extra seats?? Impossible!!

Skin Totally Healed

Now comes the part why I believe we were allowed to go. A nice man was sitting next to me. I could not help but notice the skin on his arms looked almost mutilated. We began to talk and he told me he spent months in a hospital in Vietnam trying to recover from this horrible skin disease, which was contracted there. I told him how God healed our granddaughter and my son. He asked me to pray for him, which I did. We exchanged phone numbers and for several weeks I never heard a word. Then one day he called crying that he had new skin that looked like baby's skin. Our God is a miracle worker. Be encouraged to pray for the impossible. He will use you. He gave you the authority over every disease-

An Italian Consulate Healed

Another time my husband and I were touring Italy. We were in Sorrento and we were relaxing by the pool at a lovely hotel on the water. Children were loud and splashing and the mother apologized. I explained I was a music teacher and loved children. They certainly didn't annoy me at all. We began talking and in the conversation I explained how God had healed my granddaughter. She said she had never heard anything like it before. She was a teacher at a college in the states. Her husband was an Italian consulate and they traveled back and forth to Italy many times. We exchanged telephone numbers and I didn't really expect to hear from her again. Just a passing relationship I thought.

A few weeks later I heard from this woman. She was quite distraught. Her husband had been diagnosed with cancer of the voice box and she wanted to bring him to our church. We went to a Tuesday morning service. I did not get a chance to call the pastor to tell him whom I was bringing. As we sat there he walked over to her husband and said, "In the name of Jesus you are healed," and that's exactly what happened. He was healed!

They invited us to their home for dinner so we could talk about the amazing goodness of God.

The Previous Dream

As we approached the house and I walked up the front steps. I recalled a dream I had of the identical house. In my dream I entered the house and walked around all the rooms and I remembered the details. I thought it strange at the time dreaming about a house I'd never seen but passed it off. It's only a dream I said to myself.

It was the same house inside as well. As we walked upstairs I described this women's bedroom to her before I walked in. I described it perfectly. She was amazed and so was I. Do I understand it? No. But

I know the Lord knows all things and He will let us know how awesome He is if we will seek His face.

A Large Angel

On the same trip we were is Positano and decided to go up into the hills to see a beautiful town called Rafello. I was guiding my husband up the curving steep roads, " turn here, make a left here," just following the signs. As I told him to make a quick turn we found ourselves in this narrow, narrow alley. The car was unable to move. There were houses on each side of the alley. People were on the doorsteps shaking their hands at us. There was no use; we were positively stuck! Knowing it was my fault I started to pray. Lord please help us in some way to get out of this mess. After my prayer we noticed at the end of the alley a very very plump monk coming down towards us, swinging his rosary beads. He studied the situation and started guiding my husband backwards out of this dark alley and somehow it was working. He kept following us until we finally got out. As I was watching him he simply but positively vanished. I never really saw an angel but I know the Lord used him as an answer to my prayer. Always pray, always ask. He will be there for you, hearing and listening. You can count on it. Even in Italy.

I Heard A Voice

I was returning from a cruise, flying home from Puerto Rico. I was reading a Christian book when I heard a voice say in my spirit I want you to pray for the women seated behind you. Now, at that time I was not at all used to praying for anyone, let alone a stranger whom I had never met. I passed it off saying to myself that is only in my mind. As I heard the voice tell me again to pray, someone tapped me on my shoulder, "I've read that book," he said to me " are you a Christian?" I turned and replied; "yes" we began to talk. He lived close to me in the next town. His wife was sitting next to him. I asked if I could pray for her. He explained that she had been in pain for years; she was unable to walk on her own due to rheumatoid arthritis. After I prayed she got up to go to the bathroom still crippled still on a walker. What a failure I am I thought to myself. We exchanged telephone numbers and I didn't hear from either one of them for over a year.

Then one day I went into the travel agency I was using. There was the same man. When he saw me he was so excited repeating "you know you healed my wife. I lost your telephone number to call you with the news." When we arrived home he said she began feeling better and has not stopped walking on her own since that day. She is free of any pain.

I don't ever remember feeling so happy. Of course I couldn't heal a flea but my Jesus will use any of us if we are open and unafraid. All He needs is you. He"ll give you the words to say.

My Dear Friend

I was on a cruise years ago on the Panama Canal. I was looking at the scenery and by accident bumped into a women's leg. She was very friendly and asked me to sit down. We began to talk when out of the blue she said, " is your name Diane?" she said she had gone to psychic and the psychic told her she would be on a French ship and meet someone named Diane. I told her that psychics were against the word of god. We got a Bible and I showed her. We talked and talked; we have been best friends now for more then 20 years. God will bring into your life marvelous friends who will love you and be there for you. He will fill your life with joy and happiness.

A New Friend

God brought another very close friend into our lives about 12 years ago. My husband, mother, and I went to lunch every Friday. Sometimes we would go to a lovely place on the island. We knew the owner for years. This particular Friday they just returned from Thailand. The restaurant was empty except for 2 men seated on the other side from us. I heard one man say "I would go to church, but they would not let me sing." I said to him "I play and lead worship at my church you can sing anytime." He invited us over and explained that he had just had open-heart surgery and was having a terrible time recovering. I said, "Come Sunday. We are having a healing service" He said he would go, but we never expected to see him. When he walked into the church we were overjoyed- When the pastor began praying for people he went to the altar. My husband was ushering at the time. He said, our friends' back was on fire. He fell out in the spirit on the floor, which happens to people when the power of god comes on them. It has happened to me.

He got up and was healed. He is an elder of the church now. He prays for many people and leads countless people to the lord. God is using him mightily. He and his wife are very close friends.

Any young people who might be reading this, God will bring the friends into your lives that will be there for you. Wonderful friends whom you can count on. Make no mistake about it. He loves you and will watch over you in everyway. Seek Him, He will show you He is real. He will come into your life and you will never be the same.

As the years have gone by I have become very close to many of my students. I stay close to them even when they go to college.

I Won!

I love all of my students as if they were my own. Some of them stay with me from the time they are five or six until they are seniors in high school. We become very close and they share many things with me.

Just recently one of my younger students and I somehow got on the subject of prayer. She was going into a New York state competition as a gymnast. She asked if I would pray that she would win. I had answers to prayer when I was competing and I was thrilled to pray for her. She also prayed before competing and her prayers were answered, she did win. I was overjoyed and her mom said I was the first one she called with the news!

I taught her how to pray- Father, in Jesus' name and I am sure that the Lord will use her in a mighty way, as she grows older. What a blessing to be able to speak to young ones about the power. Never let an opportunity go by when you might be able to encourage someone; especially young people, because it could change their life.

A Student Passes Tests

Many of them have no religious upbringing and it seems I always get them interested when I tell them I will pray for them. Such was the case with a young man I was teaching. He told me of a test he had to take which he couldn't possibly pass. I would definitely pray for him I said. He called me during the week to say he passed. Needless to say it became my job to pray for mostly every test and his marks started improving.

His mother called me and I began sharing with her what I had experienced about Gods power. We became friendly with his parents. We went to dinner a few times. His dad was a pilot and a very lovely man, not very interested in god though. We were invited to this boys Bar Mitzvah, we were delighted to attend.

Please Pray For My Dad

About 6 days before the affair, I received a telephone call from my student. His dad was in traction in the hospital from a previous back ailment. He would not be able to attend his Bar Mitzvah. I began asking the lord to heal him but he got progressively worse.

We arrived at the country club and to my surprise his dad greeted us as we walked through the door. He told us this story; I was in terrible pain from the moment I arrived at the hospital. I was constantly on painkillers throughout the night and day. This morning I was so depressed not to be able to be with my son. I wish I could have prayed but I didn't know how. All of a sudden I was lying in bed with my legs in the air. Heat came into my whole body. All the pain vanished and within one hour I checked myself out of the hospital and here I am.

No More Time

After that incident he was very receptive to everything I told him about the Lord. He kept saying he wasn't ready to become a believer. I kept praying for him knowing that he had difficulty making any kind of a commitment.

One day flying down to Florida his plane crashed and he was killed. I never saw my student again. God gives us a chance- We really never know when He is going to call us home. Never put off asking him into your life. Its so easy, " Jesus forgive me of my sins. Come into my life; be my savior and my lord." That sentence changes everything! Everything! That's your ticket into heaven- accepting him as your savior and lord and putting Him first in your life!

Take Off The Brace

Another student wore a brace on her hand but still kept taking lessons, and was still able to play. This went on for weeks and one day I simply said' " let's pray for that hand to be healed." She took the brace off and never put it on again. Her mom came in the next day with a gigantic tray of candies and nuts. Of course I wanted nothing. I had been given the privilege of praying for her and my God healed her and she is still healed to this day. Praise his name!

How wonderful it is for Him to use us. Lots of times I think I'm on an assignment, His assignment, and I'm thrilled when the outcome is victory! Of course all the praise and glory goes to Him!

Nothing's To Difficult

One of my adult students came in for a lesson and said she would be stopping lessons for a while. She came in hunched over in excruciating pain, explaining that she had a slipped disc and it started giving her so much trouble.

I told her of God's miraculous healing power. "I'm not a believer," she replied. I asked if I could pray" she said "of course." She left the same way she came in, hunched over. By now I realized God always answers prayer, but sometimes it takes awhile to see the result. I certainly was only the human vessel being used.

The next morning her husband called. I did not know him. He told of her unbelievable recovery. She couldn't even hold her toothbrush before. He asked me to explain what happened. I said, "I believe the Lord touched her." Did I want them to come to my church?- no not yet. Begin reading the Bible- Learn of Him! You will learn to love Him as He loves you. That's just what they did, read for hours and hours. Then they came to church a beautiful loving caring couple and God blessed them and their family.

Do I understand why God might heal an unbeliever and yet wonderful Christians, whom I have prayed for over and over again, die? No I don't. I only know He is sovereign and if you put Him first in your life, He will under no circumstances let you down. He'll show you he is real- The coincidences will be happening to you- "Can this be God?" you'll say-of course it can. You'll find Him everywhere; Signs are everywhere, Just look for them.

You're a Believer?

My dad was taken to the hospital. He had water in his lungs and needed a pacemaker. While he was in intensive care a woman was in the bed next to him. It appeared she was in a coma- Her family was around the bed. I suspected she was not doing well. Then a priest came in, He looked at me and said, "You're a believer, come and pray with me." How he knew this I did not know. He asked the family to leave for some reason. We prayed together and I left. The next day the woman was eating breakfast. I was stunned! She explained to me that she had leukemia and last night she felt heat go through her body- Exactly when we prayed. She was released from the hospital and I stayed in touch with her. She was totally healed- What could be better?

A Friend Came To Know Him

My husband invited a man from work over one day with his fiancée. He had an unbelievable sense of humor and we instantly became friends. He was a nonbeliever and poked fun at the different miracles and healings that were taking place in our lives. " Who is getting out if of the wheelchair this week?" He would say, It really didn't affect me as he didn't know any better. "Don't mock and criticize" I would say. "Someday you might need the Lord."

Cancer struck our friend in his lungs and spread to other parts of his body. He wasn't given much hope of survival. I prayed for him constantly asking the Lord to touch him. Six months was the prognosis.

One day he asked me if I would pray for a private part of his body to be made normal. It had doubled in size. I replied, " I think that's something you should pray for." The doctors said he would have to live that way for the rest of his life.

He really did not know how to pray but said to the Lord "Jesus I don't know you and you don't know me but when you were on earth would you have wanted to walk around like this?" He said, " Jesus if you are real please heal me," and in the morning everything was normal.

Given Added Years

He, of course, became a believer and even gave out Jesus t-shirts in the hospital. I wish I could say that the cancer disappeared but it didn't. However, God extended his life for many years and he never died of cancer. He was always cheerful, always funny; always up- I surely miss him. I will see him again. I will walk the streets of gold with him because I know for sure where he is. Always tell everyone about the savior. It might be you who causes them to walk through those beautiful gates on streets of gold.

God Made A Way

Although my son had a miraculous healing he never did well in school and when he graduated from high school he worked a menial job as a painter for my son-in-law's firm. I knew in my heart that God had something better for him so I kept asking Him each day for a better position. One morning I had a Christian station on. A woman said "there is a woman praying for her son to better himself in life." She said "her prayers are going to be answered." When the program went off, an advertisement came on for the Grumman Institute of Technology. As I don't believe in coincidences, my son and I went there so he could take a test for computer programming. After finishing the test, the administrator sat us both down in his office. "The highest score in this category is 90 and you got an 89- the highest score in this category is 21- you got a 19," he continued. When he finished he said, "you are accepted, you can start next week." Joy isn't quite the word that I felt. He graduated eighth in his class and landed a job in Gibbs and Cox in the city as a computer operator.

We were elated- He was a wonderful young man with a fabulous personality and he loved God with all his heart. Life was wonderful; all was well.

I heard somewhere that prayer is earthly permission for heavenly influence. In my life that sentence manifested itself many many times.

God throughout it all has been faithful to me. He's been my strength, my comfort, and my peace. No matter how bleak it looks, no matter what the situation, turn to Him. He will either remove the problem or He will be by your side as you go through it.

A Braham's Concerto

We always were a very close family. My son loved his sisters and my brother's children who lived next door. We always were together.

One day he and I went shopping in the mall. I was looking for a Brahms concerto that I loved. I didn't know the name of it so each time we went into a music store I would hum the melody to the clerk. This embarrassed Rick so much that he ran out of each store. When he got home he told everyone how ridiculous I was humming in the store. You are probably wondering why I put this in the book, but later on I will tell you this was significant, and how the Lord used it to comfort me. He will use anything to let you know he is real- a song, a bird, a plant, anything. Get ready- signs follow those who believe.

Jesus Blessed My Business

I would encourage anyone who is reading this book to put the Lord at the head of your business. I really never had an opening in my schedule that wasn't filled by eager new students. One day I asked the Lord, "Is it you Jesus that beings all these students to me? Please show me."

One day a girl by the name of Shari Fish did not want to practice piano anymore and her mother Evelyn Fish called me to say she'd be stopping lessons. Her lesson was Mondays at 4:30. Unusually I had no one waiting for her spot. The next day the phone rang. "This is Evelyn Fish," she said. I replied, "oh, did Shari change her mind?" "What do you mean?" she said, "change her mind about what?" She explained her daughter Shari had never studied with me before and she did not know the other Evelyn Fish. I asked if Mondays at 4:30 would be suitable? " How did you know? Mondays are my only day off" so Shari Fish moved into Shari Fish's time slot. I knew the answer. He oversees everything and will bless us beyond belief if we put Him first in our lives. He is still blessing my business and I have been teaching for more than forty years.

The Lord has used me to help my students many times.

The Real Demon

I had a student who had many problems and was suicidal. He was a lovely young man and we discussed God many times. We became close. I prayed for him, as he really believed a demonic power was living inside of him. He called himself Mandrake. My student was hospitalized quite a few times trying to commit suicide. He told me he fought with this demon. He told me how this demon would beat him and throw him to the ground- I had come in contact with a demon's voice and believed him. The situation got worse, I was praying for him everyday. Then one day he told me that the demon did not like coming to lessons. He was afraid of me he said. I knew from the word that we as believers have power over Satan. The Lord has given it to us. I simply called him out in Jesus' name and he obeyed- "he's gone!" my student replied, and he was! I see him now and then and he's perfectly well. Praise his name forever.

Demon Speaks Over T.V.

My middle daughter was home from school when she was in high school- we were cuddling in bed watching a Christian program in the morning. I was telling her the importance of a Christian life while you are young. She said, " Oh mom, you're much too strict about Christian values." The T.V. went blank and all distorted and a voice unlike I've ever heard- low husky and demonic came over the airways and said "I can come and take over your house and your family anytime I want." I replied, "You have no authority in this house, in Jesus' name you must leave." The Christian program returned as simple as that. We have power over Satan. Jesus has given us the authority. All we have to do is use it! That was many years ago and my daughter and I still recall when a demon spoke to us out loud over the T.V. Be careful what comes into your house over the airways. Satan is seeking to destroy you and your family. He told us plainly he wanted to do just that!

There Were Two

We were invited to a party in New Jersey. My friend worked at the U.N. and asked us to attend. Her daughter had tried to get pregnant for years and years to no avail. Then she tried invitro. She was very nervous that it would not work. She and I excused ourselves and went into the bedroom and prayed that the Lord would give her a baby. A few weeks later she called and told me the great news. I was thrilled for her. I knew God answered our prayer.

A Baby Lost

However, about a month later she called telling me that she was having a miscarriage. We prayed again, but she lost the baby. Then we found out how truly amazing God is. She lost the baby, but there were twins and the other baby survived, and is fine and healthy today. Praise his name forever, He will never leave you.

I'll Be The First to Go

One Saturday evening our friend and his wife came to visit. He didn't know the Lord at this time. We believe that Jesus is coming back and that we will be taken up to heaven with Him before the great Tribulation. Our friends used to kid us all the time saying when we leave he would move into the house because he had an apartment. He said to Rick, " don't go with them," jokingly, " I'll teach you how to be a dealer in Vegas and you'll make alot of money." Ricky replied "if the Lord comes back I'll be the first one to go." That night at twenty-one years old Rick went to sleep and didn't wake up- My son-in-law said that night Rick said to him, "my work on earth is finished. My whole family accepted Jesus because of the miracle of my birth." Of course my son-in-law told me this after Rick went home to the Lord.

Twenty One Years Were Up

After all the healings and miracles the Lord had done in my life this was something I couldn't understand. I was needless to say, devastated. Losing a child is unlike anything you can imagine. The grief is unbearable. There's no place to go, no place of peace- my girls, my husband, my mom, my family were just broken.

The Pit

Each night I felt like demons were taking me down into a pit- I couldn't sleep and I couldn't get out of that pit no matter how I tried. Night after night I was being tormented. Mentally tormented! It was difficult for me to pray. I was struggling to keep my faith, but somehow the gold teeth that my mother received helped me through. There was absolutely no explanation for the gold in her mouth. It could have only been from God. I knew where my son was. I knew he was with the Lord but not seeing his face each day was unbearable. It seemed it was all I could think about. It engulfed my days and nights. Everyday I sat in the backyard waiting for some sign, any sign, signs did come but not then.

The Letter

One day in the midst of all the pain and sorrow a letter came from a minister to whom I had never written and never sent money. I don't know how he ever found my address or my name. He wrote, " Dear Diane, I know what it is like to go into the pit. I was there when I lost my mother. You don't have to go into that pit anymore. Begin taking you eyes off yourself and start helping and praying for others." I was astounded. How did he know what I was going through unless the Lord showed him? It gave me new hope. I definitely did what that letter told me to do and little by little I left the pit and was able to sleep again. Praise His name.

A Book With His Face

I began teaching again when the children started school but it was hard to concentrate. Grief is consuming. One day while I was teaching I said to the Lord, "I just can't do this anymore-Please show me that he is OK." When I prayed that prayer a student came over from the waiting room and said "someone left this book on the table." It was a pocketbook and on the cover was a blonde woman playing the piano and a young man was leaning on the piano looking at her. The title was, " Love in another key." The young man had an argyle grey sweater and grey pants. It's the outfit we had given our son for Christmas. It was the picture of Rick and I realized the Lord was trying to tell me my son loved me still, but in a different way- love in a different key- as a music teacher it certainly hit home- I looked in the book and it belonged to a student who was from my church. I called her mom and she said I should keep it and she would buy it from the library. I have it framed on my wall in the kitchen with Rick's picture above it. Every time I look at it I'm reminded of where my son is. Walking on the streets of gold-

God Sent A Bird

It was the beginning of many signs, all of which I praised the Lord for. The next strange thing that happened took place in the middle of winter. I was teaching a friend's daughter when all of a sudden a bird began pecking at my music room window, which is about six feet long. He started at the top and pecked and pecked all the way down. We looked at each other in amazement. The bird stayed all afternoon, all week and all month. If I was in the kitchen he'd come to that window and perch. If I was in the bedroom he came to that window and pecked. It was quite an unusual sight. I didn't attribute it as a sign I just thought it strange. He stayed and stayed all winter and one day he was gone.

A Bird Comforted A Pastor

I was in church one Sunday and the pastor in the middle of his sermon said "if God has to He will send a bird to comfort you and explained how a bird came to him each morning. Even though I've heard and read many stories about birds coming when a loved one dies. I don't know for sure it was from the Lord. I hope it was. It comforted me.

A White Dove

I've had other experiences with birds- my husband and I read the bible in bed every morning. One morning while I was praying I heard the Lord say. "I'm going to send a white bird to comfort you" I told my husband what He said. Again it was winter and I passed it off. The next morning there he was sitting on the wire outside our bedroom as white as snow. I think the Lord does these things in our lives to let us know He is with us, watching, caring, protecting. I have certainly come to realize that nothing is a coincidence with God. That the creator of the universe sends a white bird to land on the wire outside my bedroom completely astounds me.

A Sign In The Sky

The Lord sent many other signs that my son was with Him on the streets of gold. I was in church soon after he passed and I asked the Lord to show me a sign in the sky- I don't really know why. When we returned home I looked up and the sun was pulsating. That's the only word I can think of to describe it, pulsating. It was a sight. The next day we read about the phenomenon in the newspaper- I'm certainly not saying that everything you ask God for He will do but He did these things for me and He's still doing them. Thank you, Lord.

Whenever I would get in a depressed state I'd go to mom's room and say, " Mom let me see those gold teeth." She showed me and somehow I was comforted knowing the only one who could have done such a miracle was God and my son was with Him in heaven and I will see him again.

The Brahms Concerto

The first anniversary of losing Rick we went to an inn in Pennsylvania just to get away from our house and that atmosphere. I knew that the Lord would do something for me that day. The day was quite uneventful; we shopped around, looked at antiques and kind of took our minds off the situation. At night we went to dinner and as I picked up my fork the music went on and the song was the one where he was with me when I went from store to store humming Brahms's Symphony. I had not heard it again since that time. Every time we hear it, we will know all is well

If You Could See Me Now

Another time we were in a place called Cold Spring on the Hudson River and as we drove down to the river I had this overwhelming feeling that Rick could see us that he was close. With that a song came on the radio, the words were " if you could see me now walking on the streets of gold" and then we lost the station. I went into the town and asked a woman in one of the stores what was the Christian station on the radio. She said, "Oh, there is no way you can get that station here, its too far away" I explained to her what happened. She looked up the telephone number of the station. When I got home I called and yes they were playing that song and sent me the tape, which I still have to this day. "If you could see me now." He knows our hearts. He sees every tear, he cares.

Not In His Plan

What I didn't quite understand is, if the Lord loved me how could I have gone through so much pain and grief. It didn't seem possible that he would allow me to suffer so much. However, as the years passed I realized that God is still the same. He still listens to my prayers and still answers. Recently I asked him, " Lord why couldn't Ricky be here with a house and a family like my girls?" I heard in my spirit plainly "it wasn't in the plan" simple, it wasn't in the plan. I said is over and over again and since He is the ultimate planner it kind of made sense to me.

The Signs Continued

I thought the miracles and healings would stop with his passing and it seemed that the Lord was always mindful of my pain and would do different things to remind me that my son was okay.

Another Sign

We went on a short cruise one year around the time of his going to heaven. I asked the Lord, "please show me all is well." There was a beautiful grand piano in the center of the ship. I started playing music that I played in church. People gathered around and started singing, before long I was praying for people, I was amazed.

That night I was asked to play again, five lovely dressed African-American women came over to the piano. One asked me, "do you play gospel music?" she added that she was a gospel singer on a radio station in Baltimore. We started playing and singing and the other four women did the background. The casino was in the round above the piano. All the sounds of slot machines stopped. People were around the balcony praising the Lord- We played and sang for over an hour. It was marvelous, people wanted to know how long we had been performing together. God does things like that, things you'd never expect, and usually in my life He doesn't do the same thing twice.

Seven Blooms

However, every year on August seventh when my son went to heaven, the Lord does something special. It's always something I would never expect. I have a Cereus plant that blooms once a year, it looks like a large orchid and its smell is incredible. It fills the house, if it gets one or two blooms every summer I am thrilled. They are so spectacular, on August seventh two or three years ago, seven blooms opened on the same day on the same plant. I said thank you to the Lord- it was my sign- Especially for me. He knew what to do.

Hit By A Car

About six months after my son went to heaven my middle daughter was working in the city. She called to say she was on the train and would be home shortly. An hour went by and then two hours, I began to pray for her safety. I prayed for quite awhile when the phone rang. It was a police officer. He said, "do you believe in miracles?" I said "of course!" "Well," he said, " you just had one. A hit and run driver hit your daughter coming off the train. If the car wasn't so low she would have been killed. She's at the hospital for brain trauma." When we got there they were taking glass out of her hair and clothes. It's a sight no mother would ever want to see. That began several weeks of unbelievable stress. Our phone would ring every night she would say, "mom they're trying to kill me, I hear them coming." The medication they were giving her for a scar on her brain was certainly not agreeing with her. She would hallucinate at all times, and use all kinds of profanity. It just wasn't my daughter. We begged them to change medication but to no avail.

We Signed Her Out

Her leg was in cast. One morning while we were in church there was a telephone call from the hospital saying the doctor was going to operate on her leg. My daughter had told the doctor that she was a professional ski racer and had to have immediate surgery. We raced to the hospital and explained to the doctor my daughter had never skied.

My husband and I had decided to take matters into our own hands. We got a wheelchair, pulled the car to the back entrance, never signed her out of the hospital and took her home. The lord would have to be her healer- it took a few weeks, but she returned to her normal loving self. She has slight problems from the accident, but she forgave the person who hit her. She's a strong, wonderful mother of 3 beautiful children and god has given her a beautiful man of god as her husband. Sometimes we go through pain and suffering but he brings us out stronger then we were before.

Out Of The Coma

About 3 months after the car hit our daughter my mom was coming home from shopping and hit a tree. She had over 100 stitches in her face. When I got to see her she said she didn't even have one pain. Her face looked like a road map; it certainly looked terrible.

Across from my mom in the hospital there was a woman who appeared to be in a coma of some sort. One day a young woman came to her bed and was crying. I went over to her and asked what the problem was. She explained she was from Georgia, her mom had been this way for several weeks. I wanted to encourage her, so I began telling her about my moms gold teeth. The women in the coma sat up much to our surprise and was listening quite intently. When I said that we would be walking on streets of gold in heaven as the scripture says she simply closed her eyes with a smile on her face and died. Was that the hope she needed to hear before she went to the lord? I do not know. Maybe someday I will meet her in that glorious place and she will tell me- for now I can only guess.

Love Worshipping

I was on the altar leading worship for many years. It was my passion to play for the lord. It was probably the most fulfilling time in my life. I love when people worship to the music I was playing. I promised the lord that if anyone was at the altar for prayer I would never leave the organ and I never did.

A New Baby

During this time my younger daughter had a very difficult time getting pregnant. I was praying for her everyday, asking god to intervene. "when she gets pregnant," I said to Him, "I will run around this church in humility and thanksgiving." When that most happy day occurred, jubilant though I was, I couldn't run around the church because I was on crutches.

Dealing With Cancer

A growth on my left lower ankle turned out not to be a pimple as one doctor had told me, but a cancerous growth. I had to have surgery and I had 12 stitches across my artery. The doctor explained that I would have a lot of trouble putting my left foot down because of where it was sewn. I hobbled up to the altar week after week kind of saying to god, "this doesn't look good. I'm preaching healing and here I am unable to put my left foot down."

Can I Play?

One Sunday a young woman asked me if she could play the other piano across from my keyboard. Of course I was delighted and she was an excellent pianist. While she was playing I thought wow! I can get off my instrument and there will be music. I got off the altar forgetting about the crutches. My foot went to the floor. I first started walking slowly and then faster and then I ran around the church. People must have thought I had lost my mind. I really didn't care. When I got to the front of the church again the power of god hit me. When I got off the floor my leg was totally healed and I have put my heel on the floor to this day-Glory to the greatest most holy god.

Strangely that growth years later came back on my leg, just a little higher then where the cancer had been removed. But this time I did not have to have it surgically removed. I had it removed by the supreme healer and I was overjoyed not having to face that trial again. Oh yes he can do all things!

Another Growth

One day I noticed a mole in my ear. It got progressively larger and larger. I went to the dermatologist. She said it wasn't cancer but this type of mole grows and grows and if it bothers me she would remove it. I kept speaking to the mole to leave in the name of Jesus. Just as it says in the bible, speak to the mountain and cast it into the sea- I was putting on makeup one day, looked at my ear it was perfectly normal. My Jesus did it again, he's so awesome and he's given us the authority on this earth! Even over ugly moles.

Pressure Healed

Recently I had a kidney infection. After antibiotics it returned. It felt as if I was giving birth. Every time I walked the pressure was severe. I went to my doctor who gave me a thorough examination and said in essence this is how you will have to live. No need to say I was quite disturbed. That night I had on the 700 club. Pat Robertson's son said someone watching was told by a doctor, this is the way you have to live. Why don't you believe god- by His stripes you were healed. I claimed that word for myself. It took over 3 months of living with pressure and every day I would say, "pressure I speak to you in Jesus name be gone." One morning I woke up and it was gone. Never ever give up fighting for your healing- we were healed on Calvary when they beat the lord 39 times. It belongs to us- hallelujah! Ask and you shall receive. He said so- sometimes you have to be patient and keep fighting for what yours.

Forgiveness

I wanted to write a little on forgiveness. I had always been a very forgiving person my whole life. My parents had an abominable relationship to say the least. I grew up in a very unhappy home. I can't remember peace and tranquility. However I've forgiven my father for the years of stress that he caused and I pray that he is with the Lord because I believe he loved him regardless of his life.

My older brother's lifestyle was far from god like. He married and divorced three wives had three children that he still doesn't see. Whenever he was in any kind of trouble he would come to us and we opened our home and took him in anytime he needed us. I still loved him in spite of his reckless life.

When my son went suddenly to heaven. He ignored it. He sort of duped us so to speak. He would say things like, "just get over it." His coldness and unnerving attitude made me hate him. I tried and tired on my own to forgive him, but I couldn't. Many times I would hear a sermon on forgiveness and say, "yes I will forgive him" but when I left the church I realized it was a lie. This went on for months. He was living in Georgia with the third wife. One day she called to say he had a stroke. I said to my mom who was now living with us, " I couldn't care less." And what's worse I meant it.

A Radio Message

I was going to the bank one day I had a radio program on. The minister said, "so you have moved to Georgia. You are on your 3rd wife, and you are flat on your back in a hospital bed. Unless you change and forgive everybody and ask forgiveness for yourself you will not enter the kingdom of god." I knew in my heart he was talking about my brother. I came home and said to my mom "get packed were going to Georgia."

When I saw him he was totally paralyzed on one side. I always called him the playboy of the east but he did not look like a playboy now. I told him the lord sent me that he had to forgive and be forgiven. He looked straight in my eyes and said I need to forgive you first. I had answers like "didn't I hang-up your dry cleaning correctly and make your meals hot enough or entertain your girlfriends nicely?" But I found myself saying please forgive me and I'll forgive you." And the hatred was over; it was ordained by God-it left!

New Caregiver

The story isn't over. He was moved from a nursing home in Georgia to one in Long Island. His wife cared for him for a while. Then one day she told me they'd been divorced for several years and she was handing all the responsibilities over to me. Little did I know that I would be the sole caregiver. The Lord knew I would have to forgive him. His three boys never came to see him.

Passed Out

We took him out to lunch every Friday with my mom. At that time he could get in and out of the wheelchair and was able to get into the car. He is no longer able to do that.

One day while we were having lunch at a restaurant that we went to every week, his eyes rolled back into his head and he lost all consciousness. My husband tried to revive him but to no avail. His body functions were uncontrollable. We called 911, when the paramedics came they didn't even work on him. I said a simple prayer, "Lord let him live if it is possible," but your will be done.

They took him into the ambulance. He looked as if he had died and then as they were ready to leave he said. "Where are they taking me?" they could not find anything wrong at the hospital and they brought him back to the facility.

I truthfully believe that we are blessed when we encourage and care about others. Sometimes I complain about always being the caregiver for my dad, my mom, my brother, but in my heart it's who I want to be. I want to be a person who prays and supports people in need. I want to see people healed, encouraged and loved through the power of God. That is what He's called me to do. I sometimes think that God allowed my brother to live so I could be blessed by blessing him. I guess someday I'll know the answer, until then my prayer everyday is "use me."

Always There

I also have a wonderful husband who has supported me through the best of times and the worst of times. He always was there and usually he was the strong one. He's always with me when we go to the nursing home, fixing my brother's snacks and loading his refrigerator. How wonderful that I am not alone in this walk on earth. He shares in every prayer every day and therefore he shares when God answers those prayers and we rejoice together. We never move out of our bedroom in the morning without reading the word of God. If you are married, try praying together. It will change your life.

Aneurism Is Found

One day through a routine examination the doctor discovered my husband had a aortic aneurism. He told him to be always aware because if it burst he would die.

Everyday we would pray together, "Lord don't let the aneurism grow." Every time he went for a sonogram it was good news. It remained the same; this went on for three and a half years or more. Then one morning when he was going to the radiologist to check on it, we were praying and it impressed me that we were praying to the God of the universe, the creator of all things! What was impossible with Him? Nothing! I prayed, "Lord in Jesus' name let that aneurism be gone." My husband said " Babe, its been there on x-rays for years," but I really just knew that God was going to do a mighty work. He can do what you can believe Him for-

A Better Rate

By coincidence a women was coming to sell us long term care insurance. She came when my husband was at the doctor's office. We waited and waited and I got a chance to tell her some of the incidences that happened in my life. She explained that she wished she could give us a preferred rate, but being though my husband has this aneurism she was not able. The time went on and my faith went out the window. What if they took him right to the hospital I thought?

When he walked in he had a tear in his eye, which was unusual. This is his story. The doctor was examining me and asked, " what is it that I'm looking for?" my husband told him what his problem was and the doctor replied, " nothing that I can find." My husband said, " maybe it's because I have a praying wife." They would not release him until they took an MRI, as aneurisms do not just disappear. It was gone; God did an amazing work. We thank Him for it every day of our lives and P.S. we got the preferred rate. Isn't that just like Jesus, blessing His children in everyway.

God Heals A Judge

Now the story didn't end. I sold a very expensive piano and we were invited to a party given by the piano store. While we were there a voice judge who I know from judging piano for NYSSMA, the New York State School Music Association, asked if she could join us. While we were talking she said she and her husband would like to join us for dinner some evening. She first had to go for a hernia operation the next week- and she would call when she recovered. I told her what happened with the aneurism. She asked if we would pray for her and we did. That Monday my phone rang, I knew she had gone for pre-op before the surgery, scheduled for Thursday. It was her calling. "Diane," she said, "when they took the tests they could find no hernia." She couldn't understand how she who is a Jew could be healed because we prayed in the name of Jesus, and she of course, was a non-believer. I tried to explain how Jesus loves everyone and that He was a Jew himself. We did go out to dinner and I was able to tell her many of the things that happened. We will continue to remain friends. To say the least she was totally amazed at what happened and so were we.

I've prayed for people who have gotten healed and prayed for people who have gone home to heaven. There is a time appointed to us by God to die and when that time comes we will go to be with the Lord if we know Him as savior. Until that time I will never stop praying for anyone in need and I will believe that they will get well because Jesus said that we as believers should lay hands on the sick and they would recover. It's almost as if God gives me certain people to pray for as an assignment, and I take that assignment very seriously. They seem to invade my life and take over my heart!

God Heals A Nurse

Just recently I was visiting my brother in the nursing home. The woman who cares for him most of the time is an angel in disguise. She is always worrying about what he eats, what he's wearing, and even cuts his hair. I'm so thrilled to have her. This time she explained to me that she wouldn't be able to take care of him for a while. She had a hernia, which was on x-rays for ten years. The doctor wanted to operate. I told her about the judge who was healed of the hernia. She is a Christian and asked me to pray for her. We just held hands and asked the Lord to touch her. About a week later my husband and I went to visit again. She met us at the elevator exclaiming, "didn't your brother tell you?" "tell me what?" I replied, "tell you that Jesus healed me. The doctor could not find the hernia that had been there for ten years." We rejoiced together and we still get excited every time we see each other. Do not be afraid to pray for people. It is not you who does the healing. It is the Lord. He will give you the words to say. They will just come to you by the Holy Spirit. He is looking for vessels. If you ask Him He will use you and you will be mightily blessed each time someone you know gets better. There's nothing in the world more rewarding then serving the Lord.

I Heard A Voice

My niece and nephew's son got very sick. I asked my niece to write down the details so what I would be writing is accurate. My husband and I were praying for this child for a long time. Here is the account written by his mother: our niece.

One morning our son woke up yelling to us that his ankle was swollen and it hurt to walk. We brought him to the doctor right away. They did blood work but could not figure out what was wrong with him. It continued to get worse. He wound up having severe migratory arthritis through the end of that year. During one of the many doctor visits his pediatrician said he noticed a heart murmur. The cardiologist determining he had a mitral valve regurgitation, (a leaky valve) they could not determine what it was caused by. One expert felt he had Rheumatoid Arthritis. He was treated for that but it made the pain worse. Then toward the end of the spring, he was having difficulty with his fine motor skills and started having involuntary movement. In the emergency room, the neurologist diagnosed his neurological disorder as chorea. Then his pediatrician diagnosed him with Rheumatic fever. They originally tested him for this but the blood tests were negative. The hospital did a different type of blood test and the result was positive. There is no treatment for rheumatic fever. He was medicated for Chorea and took aspirin for the arthritis pain. His heart condition was permanent. He was unable to participate in any sports and we were told to see the cardiologist regularly. We prayed all the time and asked Aunt Diane to pray for him as well.

It seemed around Christmas time that he was getting better. Then the first week in January he showed signs of the Chorea coming back. We were devastated! Something triggered a relapse of the Chorea. His neurologist gave him the medicine that he responded well to before, but this time it didn't work. The next level of medicine the doctor wanted to give him was very strong with potentially permanent side effects. We chose not to give him this medicine. His condition became so severe that he could not read or write and had difficulty walking and talking. He could not go to school and had to be home schooled. I became very emotional and depressed. I did not even call my Aunt Diane because of the state I was in.

Now I will continue telling you what happened. I called my niece since I was very concerned about her son. She explained his grave condition. I felt sure that she would have given us better news as we had been praying and praying for him. After speaking to her we left to see our children and grandchildren in Massachusetts. While we were there in the middle of the night I heard a voice and it said, "you need to pray for Robert." I don't know whether it was a dream or a real voice, but I answered, "lord if it is you we've been praying for Robert for months and months." The voice replied, "no, you need to go lay hands on Robert." That was all I heard- we were on our way home the next day. I told my husband what had happened and that we needed to stop at our niece's house. He explained we couldn't because a snowstorm was to hit Long Island by one o'clock. I knew we had to go and we did. We all prayed for him that day and I believe in my heart that healing began. Although Robert continued to get worse, my niece's faith and my faith in his healing was strong. The doctor was so frustrated with them; they would not give the medication he suggested. They knew he was going to get better, and then God confirmed his healing to my niece. While she was in church he showed her in a vision of a hand and she knew he would be healed. Slowly he began to improve. Two months later, he returned to school. At his next cardiologist appointment the doctor could barely hear the murmur and at the follow up appointment he lifted all physical restrictions. His heart had also been healed. What's impossible to the God we serve? Absolutely nothing, He is no respecter of persons. What he did for Robert and the others, he will do for you. Speak to the mountain in your life and command it to go in Jesus' name. You have the authority to do so. He has given it to you. Use it!

God Sends A Doctor

A few years ago a young woman came into my studio for piano lessons. We liked each other instantly, she is wonderful doctor and said when she walked in, "my mom died of cancer and the lord is going to give me a new mother and that mother is you." That statement startled me but since then she always was looking out for me and my husband and we are still like family. God will supernaturally bring the people into your lives that you will love and be thankful for. Good friends are treasures.

One day right before Thanksgiving she came in for a lesson. My husband had just had an entire physical and had passed with flying colors. As she was leaving the studio she wanted to say goodbye to my husband. We were leaving to go to my daughters for Thanksgiving. She asked my husband how he was and he shared how he was just given a perfect bill of health from his doctor. The only thing I have is a little gas in my throat area. Within one minute she was on the phone making an appointment for him at 2 o' clock that same day for a nuclear stress test. I was against it. We were going out for lunch but she was emphatic about it and he went for the test. The test showed a blockage in one of the arteries and he was immediately scheduled to have a stent inserted. I believe if our doctor friend would not have been there on that day my husband would have walked around with that blockage for perhaps another year. The cardiologist said that she saved my husbands life. She is also a solid believer in the Lord and knows nothing happens by chance- Gods coincidences are his handiwork and if you watch for them they will happen to you all the time. Just always be aware. He is always at work.

A Tumor Leaves

One day my daughter called upset that a doctor found a tumor in her breast. She had to make an appointment with a breast doctor. We prayed together and when she went to the second doctor the tumor was gone. Why I had to go for surgery for a breast lump to be removed and she was miraculously healed I do not know. I only know that when you believe He is real and that He is all-powerful He will work all things together for your good. He said so, you can count on it. Always find someone who will encourage you and when you awaken in the morning realize how very blessed you are especially if you belong to

Him. I want you to know that he is interested in every part of our lives not only our health but our finances, our dreams, and our desires.

Where's The Diamond

My husband of 51 years bought me a diamond ring for our engagement. I've worn it all these years and I have other diamonds my mom had given me set around the engagement diamond making a rather large but lovely ring. I decided to have it appraised one day and was shocked to find out that it was worth close to ten thousand dollars. I thought I would get it insured in case I ever lost it. Before I had a chance to do that I discovered one morning that the stone was missing. It really wasn't the money that bothered me but I certainly had a sentimental attachment to it. We looked everywhere but it could have fallen out anywhere; the bank, the supermarket, the car, etc. The woman who cleans for us came and also searched the house. We looked in every vacuum cleaner bag. She scoured the house to no avail.

I really had no faith to pray to find my diamond. I didn't ask the Lord. At this time we were having our house painted, different rooms at a time. I was witnessing to this painter of all the things the Lord had done in my life. He was coming on a Sunday to paint the last bedroom in our house.

While we were at church my granddaughter and grandson who lead worship began singing a song, which I had played all the time. Its name was "our God is an awesome God." While singing it dawned on me my God is awesome!! He can do everything and anything and I asked if he could bring me back my engagement diamond. When we came home my husband took off his shoes, which I have never seen him do, ever-He said to the painter, "Come I will show you the room." It was the last bedroom of our house which neither one of us go into. It's used only as a guest room. When he came down he had a smile on his face-" is this what you were looking for?" he said. The diamond was stuck in his bare foot. When these things happen to you, you know that the creator of the universe cares about you- Not only physically, but everything that you hold dear and nothing is by chance, nothing! It's his handiwork. Begin looking for him to work supernaturally in your life. He wants a relationship with you.

Summa Cum Laude

My brother had called me and asked me to pray for a daughter of a friend of his. I started writing to her and told her many of the things that Jesus had done in my life. I've come to realize that many people even Christians in the church have no idea about the power of the Lord. They don't hear it in church. People in my own church were amazed when I shared some of the experiences I have had. That is why I think it so imperative that you tell everyone, who will listen, what the Lord has done for you.

This girl confided in me about some of the horrendous things that had happened to her. She was very distraught although she was quite innocent. She couldn't understand that our Lord is a God of grace and forgiveness, no matter what we have done. I wrote to her many times about Jesus.

She got better and eventually went back to college. I just was told that she graduated Summa cum Laude. Her mother told my brother that I changed her life. That statement made me realize that God is looking for people who will be obedient and reach out to others to encourage them that with the help of the Lord they can make it. Everything is possible with Him. I cried for a while to think that he used a nobody like me. I'm blessed- please let Him use you. You will never be sorry. He will bring you people that you never knew existed.

I've Got The Ticket

While traveling in Europe, we met a lovely couple while on a river cruise in Germany. We met at breakfast in Amsterdam. She was a nurse and he was a writer and shared that he has several books on the best sellers list. He asked me what the book I was writing was about. When I said it was about the amazing things Jesus had done in my life. He said, " oh no! You're not one of those born agains are you?" I said, " it doesn't matter that you don't believe we can still be friends." I did not witness to him on the cruise, but his wife was open. I liked her immediately and told her many things that had happened.

When we retuned home they came to our house and we remained friends.

A Brain Tumor

Then one day the phone rang, and it was him, which was rather strange. He explained that he was diagnosed with a brain tumor. I told him I would certainly pray for him. It started a lovely relationship and I began telling him about the Lord. He started to be open to it. I explained accepting Jesus as your savior was your ticket into heaven. A couple of days later he said to me, " I have the ticket," and then I learned he passed away. Would I have loved to see him healed- absolutely! But God had other plans. Now he is walking on those streets of gold- to think God can use you to open those pearly gates for someone to enter in is positively awesome. Don't keep it to yourself. Give it away! Tell them!

His Wife Believes

Recently his wife told me she accepted Jesus as savior and Lord and said it was no coincidence that we met. It was all in His plan, praise his wonderful name. How many people will we meet there that we influenced?

A Winter Plant

One weekend in March we were going up to Massachusetts to spend time with my daughter and her family. We brought a turkey with us. My husband who is now the cook in our family and a mighty good one, I can add, said "lets stop and get celery, carrots, and onions for the turkey." It was Saturday, very crowded, and I did not relish going food shopping. However, of course I was on line with many others with my vegetables. On the way out I noticed a fantastic plant in the flower section. I thought I owned every species of plants but this one was very unusual and I thought, you are going home with me. However, looking back at the express line I decided to leave the plant there rather than wait.

On arriving home we had a snow and rain mixture. I began teaching piano the next day. I have ceiling to floor windows in my studio. I looked out at the garden, which was lightly snow covered and quite bare, and there to my utter amazement was that unusual plant growing in the snow quite large and very healthy.

Is God concerned about everything in your life even an insignificant plant? You can bet your last penny on it. He loves you! He cares; He knows and He will do things for you and you alone that no one else will even believe or understand. Trust him, be His friend. He waits for you everyday to talk to Him, to lay down your burdens and to be your loving father and intercessor.

In The Name Of Jesus

Does the Lord hear and answer immediately? Yes sometimes, I believe he does.

My granddaughter was taking horseback riding lessons and invited us to see her ride. It was like an arena, she was riding beautifully and something must have spooked her horse. The next thing I knew she was on the ground her foot caught in the stirrup. The horse was going around in circles. I yelled at the top of my lungs- In Jesus' name – In Jesus' name. Her foot came out of the stirrup and she was freed. Do I believe that the Lord stepped in? You better believe it. The name of Jesus is very, very powerful and praise his name. He gave that name for us to use.

Kidney Stones

Wherever I go I try to share my faith and what God has done in my life. A young girl blows out my hair for me after I get it colored, I have had white hair for years, but as I got older it certainly made me look older. This girl was telling me how she was in and out of the hospital because of Kidney stones. She said they were very painful and her doctor said she would have to have them removed. I told her my husband had kidney stones and one time I laid hands on him in Jesus' name. He passed the Kidney Stones and never was bothered by them again. She was interested and I kept speaking to her about the power of prayer. She said she was a believer. I told her speak to the mountain in this case kidney stones. She was so excited of the prospect of getting healed. I did not hear from her but the next time I went her face said it all! The Lord had touched her; the doctor told her there were no stones to be found. It really wasn't that amazing to me, because of that healing this girl wanted to know more about the Jesus who touched her. The Lord has a purpose for everything even Kidney stones.

Triplets

As I am drawing to a close a marvelous miracle has happened. My husband and I were praying for our granddaughter and grandson to have a child. They both lead worship at our church. They are a young wonderful couple who love God with all their hearts. However, for a long time conception did not take place.

Great News

And the amazing news, she was pregnant not with one child, that would have been incredible but with three. You see God will do more than you can think or imagine. When nothing seems to be going your way ask Him and He will step in and you will know without a doubt that He is real and that He loves you no matter what you've done or who you are. We are now looking forward to becoming great grandparents. I can't still believe it.

The Doors Opened

I believe that God will go to great lengths to speak to you and encourage you, and that He does hear and does answer prayers.

I am very very close to a young man in our family. He and his family have been very very good to my younger brother whom I love dearly.

This young man was fired from the position he held which was a high paying job. He was supporting my brother, his family and has a beautiful home.

I began praying every day and sending him encouraging Emails that the Lord is amazing and all things are possible with Him. Everyday my prayer would be, "Dear Lord open the door and bring him a new position." I prayed for at least nine months that my prayer would be heard, I believed it, but there was no answer.

My family went to a hotel to celebrate my daughter's birthday. My son-in-law arranged for the girls to have massages-much to my delight. When the woman came out to call me I knew immediately that she was a Christian. We began talking about what the Lord had done in our lives. She told me amazing things and I in turn also witnessed to her about my mom's gold teeth and other testimonies.

Then she stopped massaging and said to me you are praying for a young man for a long time that the doors should open. I began to cry, " Lord you are giving me a message on a massage table? How strange is that?"

When I arrived home- this message was on my computer from my nephew. " Praise God, the doors just opened- I have a new position." Was it my prayers that brought this new job? I don't know. I only know pray without ceasing. Speak to the mountain, God had given you the authority use it and believe! This young man's wife is my niece- the Lord touched her as well.

Healed Of Acid Reflux

This is a testimony written word for word by my niece whom I am very close to.

Ever since I was a young child I enjoyed anything with spices. After consuming cases of hot sauce and spicy food I ended up diagnosed with acid reflux at age fifteen. It was not called that at that time. I would ingest at least three full bottles of Tums within a month. As I grew older the pain seemed to increase. I still was eating spicy foods. Eventually the reflux was so bad I was prescribed stronger medication that I was to take one time a day for the rest of my life. I did not like being dependent on medication for any reason but it was helping me. I did not have a choice in the matter as the burning kept increasing in my throat. It was my Aunt Diane's stories about speaking to the problem that got me thinking. I must admit I was never a miracle person. I believed in them but never experienced such a thing myself.

Around 2am I had a very bad episode of the reflux. I sat up in bed crying from the pain. I kept hearing my aunt say speak to it. I very loudly said if my aunt can do it why can't I? I am done with acid reflux, I am god's child and I refuse to have you in my body anymore. In Jesus' name you have to go! Amen. I went back to bed. The following morning I went to grab my pill, I stopped and said no. I prayed and I believe what I said. Since that day I have not had to take any prescribed or other medication relating to my acid reflux. I keep the bottle as a reminder that if we actually believe and God said He would do it then its time we start asking Him and speaking to our problem! I am thankful every day-

A Sign

I became friendly with one of my students mothers, a lovely Asian woman who was always interested in my stories about the Lord. I shared many things with her but she never was convinced He was real.

One day she took a trip back to China to see an ailing parent. On the plane a man sat next her and started a conversation. He told her he was a pastor of a church in China and he was returning home. She began telling him about me and the things that the Lord did in my life. She told him she wasn't convinced that Jesus was real. She needed a sign. The pastor said, " why don't you just ask Him for one?" and he proceeded to go to the bathroom. She asked for that sign and water came pouring out of the ceiling on her head. She asked the stewardess where it was coming from. No one could answer her. When the pastor returned she told him what happened. His answer was what sign did you think the Lord could have given you in an airplane?

Do signs really convince people that God is with us? I do not know. The signs He's given me and is still giving me touches my heart. He is such a loving God.

Now what is strange about water on the plane is this:

I have been going to the same hairdresser for sixteen years. I tell her everything and I shared this story with her because I have been telling her about Jesus for years, wanting so much for her to go to church with me, which is very close to the beauty shop in Bethpage-

As I went to the desk with her to pay my bill, water just started coming down from the ceiling. We both look at each other in disbelief. She said, "It's not raining and we just had the roof fixed." Was it a sign for her as well? How do we really know?

The story continues. I believe God has a sense of humor. My hair dresser opened a new beautiful beauty parlor. When I walked in one day to have my hair done she said, "Someone stole my new sign off the back entrance." They searched for it but it was gone. Guess where they finally found it? In the church parking lot. The pastor walked into the shop and said "is this the sign?" "Yes," she replied, "It is my sign." "No" he replied, " Is this your sign to come to church?"

I'm still praying for her. I know the Lord has His hand on her life and it won't be long before she makes a total commitment to Him. Maybe she just needs another sign, you think?

Signs Are Still Happening

I read about signs from a loved one in many magazines. One sign that seems to happen a lot, people find pennies. Well, I said to the Lord there are always pennies everywhere I would ask to find dimes. I can't say I ever believed in that kind of thing before but I think when you lose someone precious any little condolence is appreciated. Well, I began to find dimes everywhere, on the floor of our stateroom, on a cruise, on chairs, on tables, everywhere. The latest, which was amazingly unusual, was to find a dime on my husband's pillow and then on my eyeglass case. Do I believe God gives a sign that our loved ones are ok? Yes, now I do. I have twenty-nine dimes collected in a little box with a scripture on it, which says all things are possible for those who believe.

I.C.U.?

Now my mom has been gone for many years. She contracted a blood infection when she was in the hospital- no matter how hard I tried I could not get her admitted to the I.C.U. Her doctor said, "Every bed is taken there is no possibility." "Really" I said. I know how to pray to someone where there is no such thing as no possibility. He kind of smiled to pacify me. I prayed Lord show me what to do- I made an appointment with the head administrator. On entering the office I saw the name of one of my student's fathers on the list of board members.

I went in and discussed my mom's problems. I stated that my student's father was on the board. That evening my mother was moved into the intensive care unit.

She recovered and we moved her to a rehabilitation center. It was lovely and she was doing quite well. One day I went to see her and she said "Diane, I'm going around and around in a circle and I can't get out." I knew Jesus was preparing me. She was about to enter the gates and not only have gold in her teeth but have gold under her feet. I replied "mom; Jesus will get you out of that circle." The next night she went home to Him.

Next to her coffin I had a picture of those gold teeth and every time someone said what's that about I said " sit down, I am going to tell you an unusual story" maybe just to encourage them that this earth is not it!

About one year after her passing I was having a barbecue. She always made great potato salad among other things. It was about eight o'clock in the morning. My husband and I came down for breakfast. I said Lord " I miss her so much, is she fine? Is she with you?" all of a sudden chimes began ringing- my husband was going out to get the paper. He turned around and said, " What was that? Thank God he is always with me when these things happen. He's my amen! It's true! There are no clocks on our wall, way to early for the ice cream man to come and we do not have a doorbell because it disturbs me when I'm teaching. Where did the chimes come from? I believe from heaven.

Then weeks later I was reading a book and one of the chapter headings was Chimes in Heaven. God always confirms to me when something like that happens.

Now after my mom passed we were in Ireland on a cruise. We were in a cemetery and a guide was explaining different things to us. There was a cross with a circle around it and he said this, you begin on the circle, when you are born, then you are baptized and you continue around the circle until Jesus takes you home. I began to cry because that was the circle my mom spoke about.

Over the years I kind of forgot about that- but just recently it was the anniversary of her death. I asked the Lord for a sign that she was well.

My husband and I have lunch at a little Italian restaurant and then usually we stroll around T.J.Maxx. This time I was in the back looking at household items and there it was in bronze; a beautiful cross with a circle around it. I cried and thanked him. He always steps in. It is now on my bench in the backyard. A tribute to a fantastic mother who constantly loved both my husband and myself; maybe more my husband but signs are precious and if we don't be careful they will pass us by. If you ask, look and keep looking. He's God; signs are easy tasks for Him. Give it a try!

Prayers can Conquer Addictions!

When I first became interested in the word of God- I listened constantly to Christian radio. The more I could learn about Jesus the happier I was. It didn't matter what minister was preaching or what he was preaching about. One day a minister was speaking about addictions. He said, " Do you know anyone who is addicted to alcohol, cigarettes or any harmful habit? Let us pray together for that person to be set free." I never realized that you could pray for such a thing. My husband had a habit of smoking. I repeated the prayer the minister prayed, asking the Lord to take away the desire to smoke from my husband. I didn't think too much about it and continued with my daily chores.

When my husband finished dinner he always lit a cigarette. This time he said, "Did you do anything to these cigarettes?" Oh my goodness I thought to myself the prayer is working. Then he opened another pack and had the same distasteful reaction. That was the last time I ever saw him smoke. Whatever the habit is that you want to break go to the Lord. Jesus has the power to set you free. Ask Him and believe! He'll help you to overcome any addiction. You'll be a new person. After trying to stop smoking for years he was finally rid of the desire to smoke. Praise the Lord!

An Alcoholic Set Free

Every year we set a very large Christmas tree up in my music room, it delights my students. It is decorated mainly with musical ornaments. Young men come every year and deliver it to our house as it's much too big for us to handle. One year we asked the young men if we could get them something to drink, meaning soda or juice. One of the men said "oh no" I am an alcoholic; I have terrible problems because of my drinking. I said to him Jesus could take the desire of alcohol away. My husband and I prayed for him. He was a very lovely young man and I felt so sorry for him.

The next year we went to pick out our tree as usual. The young man was there. "I knew I would see you again," he said. Ever since you prayed I have not had one drink. I began to cry to think one small prayer on another's behalf changes their lives forever. How dare we remain silent!

A Healing Heart

We exercise with four other couples, which have become our dearest friends. They are of different faiths and not evangelical like I am but I still like to share with them what the Lord is doing in my life.

One man who my husband and I are close to has a brother who has been very sick. I have sent him cards and emails trying to encourage him. We found out he needed a heart transplant and he was very low on the list to obtain one. We started praying that he would receive a heart. When we returned to our exercise class, which was closed for two weeks, we heard the good news that he did have the operation. A seventeen-year-old boy died in an accident and he by the grace of God received his heart. My friend explained to me that his brother was not doing well because the heart was only beating one quarter of its capacity. If the heart did not start beating normally his brother would have to remain on a machine for the rest of his life. When I left the class I began praying. My husband and I went to lunch at our local diner. My husband prayed over the food as usual and I felt that we should pray together for the heart to start beating normally- I prayed " heart begin to function. Begin beating in Jesus' name." We had lunch and returned home. Our friend called and told us the fantastic news. Out of the blue the heart began beating and he is doing well, getting better each day and will soon come home. I am writing this to tell you that your words are very powerful- would you ever want to hold back a prayer? A prayer that maybe could save someone's life. They are calling it a miracle at the hospital- was it a miracle? I don't know but I do know from many past experiences that God hears and answers. Be an intercessor you will never regret praying for others. You might bring about their miracle.

Life Triumphant

I was given the privilege of having my last couple of recitals at the Steinway Gallery in the beautiful recital hall, which is located close to my home. My students played on a magnificent Steinway grand. I was more than thrilled. At the end of the recital the manager and I began a conversation. We learned that we were both Christians and we shared our testimonies. God's people are everywhere. We were elated about the wonderful things the Lord did in our lives.

Recently I was invited to the recital hall to attend a lecture given by a professor from Julliard School of Music. Before the professor began he asked the manager if he wanted to play something. He replied he wasn't a classical pianist but he would play a piece that he wrote. He explained after Diane Dybus's recital she inspired me so much that I composed this piece called Life Triumphant. He sat at the piano and played one of the most beautiful compositions I had ever heard. It actually brought tears to my eyes. To think that what I shared with him that night caused him to compose that gorgeous music made me want to shout for joy. I don't believe in coincidences. I believe that Lord orchestrated our meeting each other.

I wanted my husband to meet him so we stopped at the gallery on the way home from lunch one day. He played the song for my husband and it blessed us both. He saw the doctor that morning because he was having some physical problems. He asked me to pray for him. I laid hands on him and I asked the Lord to heal him. The next morning he called to tell me all the symptoms were gone: I was not surprised. We are His children. He delights in healing us. Didn't He say " lay hands on the sick and they will recover?" Take Him at His word. He will do amazing things in your life.

I certainly know my work is not finished. God will send me out on many assignments to pray for people, to be an encouragement, to tell them I know for sure that there is a God above, who hears and answers our prayers who knows what we need before we even ask for it. Who loves us more than we can even think or imagine. Who will guide us, protect us, provide for us and heal our bodies. I have fantastic testimonies of what He's done and I know they will continue until He comes for us with the trump of God. I look forward to that day when the dead in Christ will rise first, I will meet my son in the air and my loved ones who have died, 1st Thessalonians 4:11. What an awesome day or night that will be. Are you waiting for Him? Are you ready? If not invite Him into your heart now, and He will live inside of you and your life will never be the same.

I've learned you do not have to be a pastor, a priest, a minister; all you have to be is a believer. He wants to use you, to tell others about Him. When you do, He will step in.